THE
EVERYTHING®

BRIDESMAID BOOK
2ND EDITION

If you ask me, being a part of a wedding—in any way—never gets old. While it may not be your wedding we are talking about right now, I still believe you deserve a congratulations. It is a big honor to be asked to be a bridesmaid in a friend's wedding. Now, as an official member of the bridesmaid club, you have a new set of duties to accompany the fun and excitement that goes hand in hand with this momentous and joyous event.

Being a bridesmaid is an experience that can test and strengthen your friendship at the same time. When you accept this position, you are acknowledging that you will be there for the bride: to lend support, to listen to her rant, to fix her train, to hold her bouquet, and to make her laugh when she needs it most.

The role of bridesmaid is not etched in stone, but with *The Everything® Bridesmaid Book, 2nd Edition* you will have the best tools to manage your bridesmaid's duties and assist your dear friend in having a wonderful wedding. So, go on and enjoy this experience.

Happy Bridesmaiding!

Holly Lefevre

The EVERYTHING Series

These handy, accessible books give you all you need to tackle a difficult project, gain a new hobby, or even brush up on something you learned back in school but have since forgotten. You can read from cover to cover or just pick out information from our five useful boxes.

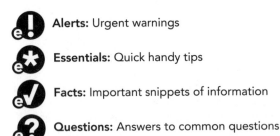

Alerts: Urgent warnings

Essentials: Quick handy tips

Facts: Important snippets of information

Questions: Answers to common questions

When you're done reading, you can finally say you know **EVERYTHING**®!

PUBLISHER Karen Cooper

DIRECTOR OF ACQUISITIONS AND INNOVATION Paula Munier

MANAGING EDITOR, EVERYTHING® SERIES Lisa Laing

COPY CHIEF Casey Ebert

ASSISTANT PRODUCTION EDITOR Jacob Erickson

ACQUISITIONS EDITOR Katrina Schroeder/Kate Powers

ASSOCIATE DEVELOPMENT EDITOR Hillary Thompson

EDITORIAL ASSISTANT Ross Weisman

EVERYTHING® SERIES COVER DESIGNER Erin Alexander

LAYOUT DESIGNERS Colleen Cunningham, Elisabeth Lariviere, Ashley Vierra, Denise Wallace

Visit the entire Everything® series at *www.everything.com*

THE EVERYTHING®

Bridesmaid

BOOK

2ND EDITION

FROM BACHELORETTE PARTY PLANNING

TO WEDDING CEREMONY ETIQUETTE—

ALL YOU NEED FOR

AN UNFORGETTABLE WEDDING

HOLLY LEFEVRE

adamsmedia

Avon, Massachusetts

An Everything® Series Book.
Everything® and everything.com® are registered trademarks
of F+W Media, Inc.

Published by
Adams Media, a division of F+W Media, Inc.
57 Littlefield Street, Avon, MA 02322. U.S.A.
www.adamsmedia.com

ISBN 10: 1-4405-0557-8
ISBN 13: 978-1-4405-0557-7
eISBN 10: 1-4405-0558-6
eISBN 13: 978-1-4405-0558-4

Printed in the United States of America.

10   9   8   7   6   5   4   3   2   1

Library of Congress Cataloging-in-Publication Data
is available from the publisher.

This book is available at quantity discounts for bulk purchases.
For information, please call 1-800-289-0963.

ACKNOWLEDGMENTS

I would like to thank the following people whose encouragement, insight, and guidance made this book possible: Amberly Finarelli at Andrea Hurst Literary Management; Katrina Schroeder and Kate Powers at Adams Media; Melissa Allen and Mary Sushinski for always sharing their expertise; Jennifer Lata Rung for providing such a great foundation; and all the vendors and brides I have worked with, who have taught me and inspired me.

Contents

The Top 10 Ways to Be a Better Bridesmaid x

Introduction xi

Chapter 1: The Who, What, and Why of Being a Bridesmaid 1

Why We Love and Need Bridesmaids. 2

Fall into Place. 4

Modern Bridesmaids, Modern Rules. 5

She Is the Bride 7

Are You Bridesmaid Material? 14

Saying No (Gracefully). 17

Chapter 2: The Maid of Honor 23

The Ultimate Maid. 24

Planning with a Friend. 27

Playing Hostess 31

Details and Duties. 33

Wedding Day Duties. 38

Chapter 3: Chatting about Cash 47

What's the Bottom Line? 48

Cost-Cutting Measures. 49

Which Way Will She Wed? 55

New Ways to Bridesmaid 59

Fashion File 65

Chapter 4: Always a Bridesmaid 73

The Pregnant Bridesmaid 74

The Newly Engaged Bridesmaid 77

So Many Brides, So Little Time 79

Confronting Your Inner Bride 81

Taming Bridezilla 84

Girl Trouble 87

Chapter 5: Fun, Fabulous Showers 93

Bridal Showers 101 94

Plan It! 96

Defining Your Options 101

The Skinny on Themes 104

Who's Coming? 113

Chapter 6: An Unforgettable
Bachelorette Party 121

The What and Why of a Bachelorette Party 122

Here's the Plan 125

Who's Who 129

Parties to Remember 132

There's No Place Like Home 135

Coed Party 140

Chapter 7: It's All Fun and Games 145

Are You a Player? 146

Game Time 148

Welcome Diversions 153

Party Like a Bachelorette 157

Playing with Props 162

Now That's Entertainment! 164

Chapter 8: Wedding Day Warm-Up........ 169

Bridesmaids-a-Lunching 170

Let's Practice............................... 171

Ways to Help (That She May Not Even
Know About)................................. 175

Stress Relief................................. 178

Great Gifts................................. 185

Chapter 9: The Wedding Day............. 189

And So It Begins................................. 190

Oh, Shoot!................................. 194

Show Time................................. 197

The Reception and Beyond...................... 203

Chapter 10: Every Wedding Is Unique 211

Second Weddings................................. 212

Gender Bender 214

The Wedding That Never Happened 216

Personally Speaking 219

Postwedded Bliss 223

Chapter 11: It Could Happen to You 229

Bridesmaid Foibles 230

Unfortunate Circumstances 234

Acts of God 236

Girls Will Be Girls................................. 239

A Family Affair 245

Appendix: Worksheets 249

Index 265

The Top 10 Ways to Be a Better Bridesmaid

1. Listen . . . really listen. Some days the bride may just need to talk things out. An open ear and a good friend are priceless.

2. Calm is contagious. Even in the most stressful moments, keep your head about you.

3. Take a break. Steal away with your friend for a simple cup of coffee—no wedding talk allowed.

4. Give your approval. This is not your wedding. Let the bride have her way on her day.

5. Speak second. Nothing is worse than listening to a bridesmaid go off on a tangent about the ugly flowers when the bride thinks they are fabulous.

6. Keep her style in mind. Plan a bridal shower and bachelorette party that pay homage to the bride's style, taste, and personality.

7. Don't compare. A laundry list of what you did better or how your friend did this or that will not make for pleasant wedding chit-chat.

8. Be agreeable. Nothing good has come from a disagreeable bridesmaid, ever.

9. Participate. You may despise the bouquet toss or wouldn't want to be caught dead line dancing, but if they are part of the festivities, get out there!

10. Behave. Dirty dancing with the groom's brother, passing out in the hall, telling off the slacker bridesmaid—not a good idea . . . for obvious reasons.

Introduction

There is no arguing: This is the bride's big day! Yes, she has asked you to be an integral part of it, but when all is said and done, your role is to assist your friend in this most special and unique time of her life . . . and hopefully have the time of *your* life while doing it!

What comes to mind when you think of being a brides-maid? Is it an image of fun and frolic with your best girlfriends, of planning showers and bachelorette parties, and walking the aisle with the cute groomsmen? Or is your vision one of tacky dresses, crazed brides, and a continuous outlay of cash? Some-where along this journey you need to ask yourself, "What does being a bridesmaid mean to me?" If you have already said yes to the bride, then being a bridesmaid should mean that you are thrilled for your friend and ready and willing to help her plan and prepare for one of the biggest days of her life.

There is no way to know exactly what your specific duties will be until you dive headfirst into bridesmaid-hood. Generally, the tone of the event and level of help and expectation are dic-tated by the bride. Sometimes, the groom gets involved . . . and sometimes so does Mom! With all of these different people and expectations, what is a bridesmaid to do? Like with all things in life, a little preparation goes a long way.

You probably have an inkling that you are supposed to help plan a bridal shower—a traditional bridesmaid duty. Oh, and then there is the planning of the bachelorette party. But that does not cover the half of it! When you accepted the position of bridesmaid, you took a silent oath to be the bride's confidant, therapist, shopping buddy, favor maker, social director—you name it; your role is to assist the bride in her wedding planning, both physically and mentally. Whether that be offering emotional support or offering your tying-bows-on-the-favors services, this is a time to step up, to be a friend, and be the best bridesmaid you can be.

Many tried-and-true bridesmaid duties are spelled out, or will be as you navigate your way through *The Everything® Bridesmaid Book, 2nd Edition*! There are some lesser-known aspects to being a bridesmaid that the bride may not even realize or know about. Can you imagine the joy on the bride's face as you offer to deliver her welcome gifts to the guests or return her rentals after the reception, or maybe, most importantly, offer to take her to coffee and for a walk to ease her tension? What about when you have her favorite breakfast delivered to her on the wedding morning? These are the things that make a bridesmaid invaluable! Yet, you must remember, errand running is a wonderful treat for the bride, but sometimes in this eventful ride, an ear that simply listens or a hug from a friend speaks volumes.

Don't fret, dear bridesmaid, you have this guide to lead you through this time, to acquaint you with the tangible and intangible aspects of being a bridesmaid. Whether you are a seasoned bridesmaid or a first timer, a primer on the essential information and traditional duties of the bridesmaids is extraordinarily helpful. The bride will thank you later.

When all is said and done, ultimately what you must remember is that weddings are always different and always exciting. With the emotions that surround them, sometimes those experiences can be rocky, but at the end of the day, when you have stood up as a bridesmaid for your friend and offered your love and support, it is a great feeling.

CHAPTER 1

The Who, What, and Why of Being a Bridesmaid

You have been asked the question. No, not *that* question, the other big question: "Will you be my bridesmaid?" Maybe it's your best friend, your sister, your childhood pal, or distant cousin. No matter; she's asked, and you've said yes. Now you want to know what's next. And what, exactly, does being a bridesmaid mean today? Get ready to find out what this honor entails, what might be expected of you, and, most importantly, if you can fill these shoes.

Why We Love and Need Bridesmaids

To understand why we continue to need bridesmaids, here's a little historical perspective, in addition to some modern-day wisdom. With this, you can take on the role of bridesmaid with knowledge and understanding. Or, possibly, after some introspection, you may simply decide it's not for you. Either way, you'll be entering this adventure with your eyes wide open, armed with the information you need to make the right decisions every step of the way.

Position of Honor

It is a real honor that you've been asked to be a bridesmaid. Ultimately, it means that someone likes and admires you, and trusts you enough to desire your close participation in one of the most important days of her life. But are you really ready to assist your friend?

Question

What's the difference between a bridesmaid and a maid of honor?
The maid of honor generally has more responsibility than the bridesmaids, serving as the leader or organizer of the bridal party and their duties.

Many women relish, and even swoon, at the idea of being asked to be bridesmaid. The fun stuff—dresses, parties, and showers—are foremost in their minds. However, before making a commitment, you must realize that this is a job, too. The bride is looking to the bridesmaids for support, for assistance, for camaraderie, and perhaps even for their opinion and their wisdom. So, before you go out accepting every invitation that may come your way, really think about the honor that this is.

History and the Bridesmaid

There is conflicting evidence about the role of the first bridesmaids. One legend has it that in early Roman times, the bride would be accompanied by her bridesmaids as a kind of human shield when traveling to the groom's village. The bridesmaids were meant to protect her from vengeful former suitors or thieves attempting to steal her dowry.

 Fact

Even though it began long ago, the superstition of evil spirits held its ground until as late as nineteenth-century England. If you look at some Victorian-age wedding photographs, in fact, you'd be hard pressed to differentiate the bride from her bridesmaids.

The more commonly accepted origin of the bridesmaid, however, stems from superstitions held in later Roman times. In order to prevent the bride from being overtaken by evil spirits, up to ten bridesmaids—dressed almost identically to the bride—would accompany her during the wedding proceedings. This strategy was devised to outsmart the evil spirits believed to be present at wedding ceremonies.

Though the reasons have changed, the tradition has stuck. And though bridesmaids are no longer virtual twins of the bride, they are still, more often than not, twins of each other. This is most likely the result of the traditional pageantry surrounding weddings, along with the perpetuity of tradition. Of course, in recent years, more and more brides have chosen to forgo this tradition, allowing their bridesmaids to express some individuality by choosing their own color schemes or outfits.

Fall into Place

For the bride or bridesmaid who cares to do her homework, there is a long-standing history of traditional duties for those acting as bridesmaids. However, every bride is different, and so is every wedding. That means that every bridesmaid experience, and workload, will probably be different, too.

All for a Reason

Ultimately, when a bride selects her wedding party, she makes decisions for particular reasons. Her little sister may be picked because she is her little sister; her sister-in-law may be asked because, well, it is a family obligation; and her high-style BFF may be asked because she has got the bridesmaids' chops and great party-planning ideas.

Of course, this information may not be highlighted as the bride asks each bridesmaid, but it will become clear as the planning progresses. It will become apparent who has strengths where, who is there to be a family buffer, who is there to plan a fabulous bridal shower, and who is there for emotional support. Unlike the more direct duties and responsibilities, these are more intangible qualities of each bridesmaid.

Bridesmaid Duties

So what are these traditional bridesmaid duties, anyway? And what is actually expected of the typical bridesmaid? Here are some basic commonalities that characterize the role of most bridesmaids:

- Help shop for and purchase bridesmaid attire, including dress, shoes, and accessories. This attire is usually chosen by the bride, who may or may not accept the input of bridesmaids.
- Help plan, host, and pay for a bridal shower.
- Attend all prewedding parties, including engagement parties, bridal showers, and the bridesmaids' luncheon or tea.
- Help plan and throw a bachelorette party.
- Provide help with prewedding and wedding-day errands, as requested (and within reason).
- Precede the bride as she walks down the aisle.
- Be part of the postwedding receiving line, if requested.
- Do general light hosting and helping at the wedding reception, where needed.
- Provide moral and emotional support for the bride throughout the wedding planning process and on the wedding day itself.
- Purchase a wedding gift for the bride and groom.

Modern Bridesmaids, Modern Rules

While bridesmaids no longer perform the function of ruses for evil spirits or act as bodyguards against wayward thugs and thieves, they still do serve many practical functions as the bride counts down the days to her wedding. And while the duties of bridesmaids may often appear to the casual observer as nothing more than looking good for the big day, there is, in fact, much more to it . . . if the bride so desires.

The Bridesmaid's Role

There are some brides who desire nothing more than to have their bridesmaids show up in their dictated attire with hair, nails, and makeup looking perfect; these brides may be control freaks or they may already have an army of other helpers, such as the wedding coordinator, mother, or aunts, handling the shower, prewedding details, and anything else wedding related. However, there are other brides who will need you desperately during the wedding planning, for tasks ranging well beyond the traditional bridesmaid duties.

 Fact

For some weddings, you may be heavily involved in wedding planning, errand running, and other duties; for others, your responsibilities will be strictly by the book. It ultimately depends on your bride's personality and style.

For the first scenario presented here, bridesmaid-as-figurehead, you'll be expected to do little besides show up. For the bridesmaid-as-indentured-servant scenario, in which you'll be expected to perform tasks well beyond the traditionally expected (such as sabotaging the bachelor party, taking out a home equity loan to throw an elaborate shower, or to purchase that designer gown), you'll need to learn how to say no. With any luck, your experience will fall somewhere in between the two. Care to guess which end of the spectrum your role will fall on?

What's New with Bridesmaids

The new wedding party is about including those closest to you, those who are supportive and accepting and happy, to be a part of your special day, whoever they may be. Just as the role of the bride (and for that matter, bridesmaid) has evolved, so have the players who may accept that role. It is common for a bride to ask anyone she wants to serve as a bridesmaid.

❓ Question

What do you call a male friend who is part of the wedding party?
Some brides go generic and just refer to the bridal party as attendants or the wedding party. Some will call a male bridesmaid a bridesman. If he is the honor attendant, man of honor will work.

It is also common for the bride to include a close male friend in her entourage. It is no longer considered odd, taboo, or risqué to have a close male friend accompany the bride down the aisle. There may be certain aspects of the planning and the wedding day that these male friends may not be included in, such as dress fittings, bridal showers, or assisting the bride as she dresses on the wedding day, but there are plenty of ways for these new members of the bridal entourage to assist their friend as well.

She Is the Bride

There are subtle (and sometimes not-so-subtle) prewedding predictors that can help you determine just what your bridesmaid experience will really be like. Generally, the personality and expectations of the bride will dictate this experience. Be honest with yourself. If you know your friend flies off the handle at the slightest inconvenience, don't expect your bridal experience to be Zen and peaceful. Go into the experience with eyes wide open.

Working with (Not Against) Her

There are some very important aspects to this whole bridesmaid's thing that need to be adhered to. Number one: Remember, she is the bride—it is all about her (and him, too!). Number two is that it is your job to work with her. So be prepared. Answer the following questions and consult the key at the end for some clues about what you're in for in the months ahead.

1. **When she has thrown parties in the past, the bride:**
   A. Refuses to allow you to bring anything.
   B. Tells you to bring a bottle of wine or a small hors d'oeuvre, but only after you've harangued her relentlessly.
   C. Prefers BYO style, calling everyone who's invited to dictate what to bring, from the entrée to the cocktail mixers to dessert.

2. **The statement that best defines the bride is:**
   A. She's in almost daily contact with her manicurist, cleaning lady, accountant, and personal shopper.
   B. She shops only with a sister or good friend, in order to get their valued opinions.
   C. For her, shopping means raiding your closet—and frequently not returning what she's borrowed.

3. **When in crisis, the bride calls:**
   A. Her mother.
   B. Her sister or a good friend.
   C. Anyone who'll listen.

4. **Your relationship with the bride is best described as:**
   A. Respectful, but a tad distant.
   B. Equal and mutually rewarding.
   C. You are her de facto therapist.

5. **The bride envisions her wedding:**
   A. However her mother envisions it.
   B. As a starting point and celebration for a strong marriage.
   C. As absolutely perfect, or you fear she'll have a breakdown.

Interpreting your answers: If your answers were mostly A, it's a safe bet that you and the other bridesmaids will not have a great deal of prewedding responsibility. More than likely, the bride will already have legions of paid helpers at her fingertips or her mother to run the show. The best way to handle this situation is to ask before you plan. Check with the bride, her mother, her wedding coordinator, and any other involved parties before planning showers or other prewedding get-togethers.

If your answers were mostly B, you'll probably have a fairly typical bridesmaid experience, and traditional etiquette will be your guide. Expect to be involved in planning a shower or bachelorette party, as well as in other prewedding duties, as requested. Most likely, the B-type bride will be reasonable in her requests and will understand that your world doesn't completely revolve around her wedding.

If your answers were mostly C, brace yourself. This bride needs a lot of attention and hand-holding, from everyone around her. You may be at the receiving end of requests that go beyond the typical call of duty, such as scouting out vendors and caterers, running endless errands, and providing heavy-duty emotional support. All, of course, are the mark of a good friendship under normal circumstances, but beware of the bride who goes a bit too far with her demands or requests. If you're not sure as you go along, this book will help you determine which requests are reasonable and which border on outrageous.

❓ Question

May I say no?
It is an honor to be asked to serve as a bridesmaid, so seriously consider the pros and cons of declining before doing so. Read on to determine whether your reasons are suitable, selfish, or just not thoroughly thought through.

Your experience as a bridesmaid will differ, depending upon the bride and her disposition. Some brides may call you to help run errands on a thrice-weekly basis, while some may never call you at all. Some brides may need lots of emotional support during the engagement—her future mother-in-law is driving her crazy with requests; she's totally freaked about her fiancé's plans for a bachelor party in Las Vegas—and some brides may remain cool as a cucumber until she says, "I do." So the best advice, aside from fulfilling all your traditional duties, is to be flexible, patient, and always be a good friend.

Oh, the Controversy!

What? You didn't realize there could be controversy? Think again! Of course, there may be circumstances that will prevent you from being the best bridesmaid you can be. You may be tempted to say no to the bride's initial request or to go back and tell her you've reconsidered, or you may be waiting for a request to be a bridesmaid that has not been forthcoming. Tread carefully here; many a friendship has been compromised due to bridesmaid controversy.

The Surprise Request

The surprise request can come from a huge range of surprising sources—that grammar school pal you haven't seen or talked to in five years, the third cousin you've never gotten along with, or the coworker who considers you her best friend even though you're content with simply being colleagues. The surprise request will throw you for a loop, and while it's an honor that someone feels so strongly about you, it's also a commitment you're not quite sure you're up to.

 Fact

Surprised about that bridesmaid request from a long-lost friend? Consider it an excuse to reignite a waning friendship. Most likely, she feels the same way. What better way to revive a relationship?

Advice: It's never a bad idea to follow the old golden rule, and do unto others as you would have them do unto you. If you can, accept the request with grace and serve out your duties with enthusiasm. However, if you've been asked by someone you simply don't get along with (or no longer have contact with), or if you think you won't be able to fulfill your obligations, it's probably best to respectfully decline now, rather than let down the bride (and the other bridesmaids) later. Also, if you believe you've been asked for the wrong reasons—for example, she's just seeking warm bodies who can afford those designer dresses or throw a fabulous bridal shower—you may be similarly inclined to decline.

The Family Obligation

Your brother's fiancée—you're trying, really trying, to like her—has suddenly asked you to be one of her bridesmaids. Just attending the wedding, you thought, would be bad enough, now you actually have to put some effort into it. What to do?

Advice: When it comes to family, all bets are off. This person will be related to you for the rest of your life—which means there's no avoiding her, now or later. Some things are simply obligations in life, and this is one of them.

e! Alert

> Beware the bride who relishes creating a bridal "in crowd" that excludes everyone else. For some brides, forming a bridal party is akin to forming a clique in the sixth grade—a chance to publicly avenge any perceived girlish wrongs and to create new social boundaries forever captured in wedding photos.

The Poorly Timed Request

You're about to leave on your intricately planned six-month sabbatical to Europe, and your college roommate asks you to be a bridesmaid. Geographically speaking, you won't be around to help plan or attend any of the showers or preparties. Whether it's this scenario or a similar one, circumstances such as travel, pregnancy, or work commitments may prevent you from fully committing to the role of bridesmaid.

Advice: Before agreeing or declining, talk openly with the bride. Tell her your circumstances, and be honest about your level of commitment. If you know you won't be able to contribute your time, planning skills, or finances for whatever reason, let her know in advance rather than setting yourself up for unreasonable expectations just because you have a hard time saying no. Of course, most women these days have busy lives and full schedules; don't bow out just because you think it will interfere with, say, you summering in the Hamptons.

You're Totally Broke

Just out of college, recently unemployed, lost a bundle in the stock market, inundated with medical bills? Whatever the reason, you simply can't afford any extras right now—especially expenses like a bridesmaid dress, a shower, or a bachelorette party.

Advice: Once again, before declining or accepting, talk honestly with the bride. Explain your situation, she's bound to understand. Perhaps she'll offer to purchase your bridesmaid attire. Most likely, she'll be more concerned about your participating in her special day than with the money you're able to shell out. Of course, don't decline just because you would rather spend $500 on that new must-have handbag you've had your eye on. There's no doubt the bride and everyone else will see through your ruse pretty clearly.

You Haven't Been Asked

You assumed you would be asked. You have been waiting for the phone call. Yet that phone call has yet to come, and you know for a fact she's already asked two of your other friends. You're worried that maybe you're not going to be included, after all.

Advice: Give it some time. Even if she's already asked others, she may be waiting until the time is right to ask you—perhaps she wants to ask you in person. Or, if she hasn't asked anyone yet, she may have decided not to have a large bridal party. Maybe she's still deciding on the style of her wedding.

e✱ Essential

> Being a bridesmaid is not necessarily a reciprocal duty. Just because you've been a bridesmaid for someone doesn't mean you're obligated to ask her to be in your bridal party, and vice versa.

Of course, there's always that possibility that she won't ask you at all, a situation that can be dealt with in a couple of ways. If you know, for instance, that you have grown apart over the years, deep down you may recognize that your non-participation may be justified, so just accept her decision grace-fully. On the other hand, if you're completely dumbfounded by why you've been omitted from the proceedings, it may be worth talking to her (in a nonaccusatory manner, of course). Otherwise, you risk misunderstandings, and possible long-term resentment, over a situation that is often better resolved with a simple, one-time conversation. Hard as it may be, isn't it worth it to try to iron out any wrinkles in your friendship?

Are You Bridesmaid Material?

Now that your eyes have been opened wide, and you are fully aware as to what may lie ahead, the question is, will you or won't you? Obviously, the decision to be a bridesmaid is ulti-mately your own. No one can coerce you into taking on the role.

However, remember that it is an honor that you've been asked, and that the woman who's asked you obviously thinks quite highly of you. To decline is a serious step. As a woman, you've probably already realized that this type of perceived slight won't soon be forgotten.

Can You Pass the Bridesmaid Test?

You may have some very real, practical obstacles preventing you from being the best bridesmaid you can be. Mull over the following considerations to gauge whether you are prepared; then read ahead to determine what's an acceptable excuse, and what is not.

THE BQ TEST: BRIDESMAID QUOTIENT

1. **You're about to go out with your girlfriends when your newest squeeze calls for last-minute plans. You're most likely to:**
   A. Tell him yes and blow off your friends completely.
   B. Ask the guy to join you and your girlfriends.
   C. Tell him no (he called too late anyway), and ask him if you can do it another time.

2. **When friends leave you voicemail messages, your typical response time is:**
   A. They're lucky if it's a week.
   B. Usually within forty-eight hours.
   C. Almost always the same day.

3. **Your feelings about weddings are best described as:**
   A. You don't understand all the fuss, and you fully support eloping.
   B. They're great, but they shouldn't eclipse someone's whole life.
   C. The bigger and fancier the better.

4. **Your job is best described as:**
   A. You work like a dog, sixty hours a week or more.
   B. Strictly nine to five.
   C. You don't work—you're supported by your parents and/or husband.

5. **When the phone rings, you:**
   A. Screen calls, only picking up if you're in the mood.
   B. Screen calls strictly to avoid certain people (coworkers, annoying family members).
   C. Answer every ring.

If your answers were mostly A, you might need to work on your cooperation skills. You tend to do what suits you when you feel like it, others be damned (or your schedule is just so crazy you have no choice). This may put you into some hot water when it comes to being a bridesmaid, so try to put your own concerns aside—even if they conflict—if others are counting on you to be somewhere or complete a specific task. If you've given your word to do something, be sure that you do it.

If your answers were mostly B, you're openminded and know how to compromise, which means you'll probably make a great bridesmaid. You tend to see both sides of an issue, and you don't let your own concerns overshadow commitments you've made to others.

If your answers were mostly C, you're poised to become Super Bridesmaid. You tend to put others' concerns before your own, a very beneficial trait when it comes to being a great bridesmaid. You're also very enthusiastic about weddings, and you have the time to devote to helping out. Just be careful that others don't take advantage of your giving nature.

Saying No (Gracefully)

There are good excuses . . . and there are lame ones. Knowing how to distinguish one from the other is very important when it comes to making the decision to accept (or deny) a post as bridesmaid. While one excuse may be viewed as shallow and small, another may actually be a perfectly legitimate reason preventing you from serving out your duties. The key is recognizing one from the other.

Although instinct can often be your guide, there are times you may need a more objective opinion. It doesn't take a psychologist to determine what's fair versus what's just plain selfish. The following scenarios may reflect your internal rationalizations only, or they may be reasons you're thinking of presenting to the bride to turn down her request. Either way, if you're considering declining based on any of the following excuses, heed this warning: They're just not good enough.

Excuse: You don't like the dress she's chosen.

Why it's unacceptable: A bad dress is part and parcel of the bridesmaid tradition across the land. Even a decent dress may be the wrong cut, color, and style for you. A less-than-flattering bridesmaid dress is your birthright as a woman and as a girl-friend. In short, it's the last excuse for declining a request to be a bridesmaid.

Excuse: You don't like wearing dresses, period.

Why it's unacceptable: There are some things you simply have to do for love and friendship. Even if you are almost surgically attached to your jeans and Tevas, a few hours in satin and heels won't kill you.

Excuse: You'd rather spend the dress money on those cute boots you've had your eye on.

Why it's unacceptable: There are always things you'd rather spend your money on than a bridesmaid dress you'll never wear again. But sometimes our disposable income must tend toward the more obligatory.

Excuse: You're tired of always being a bridesmaid, never a bride.

Why it's unacceptable: Your day will come. And when it does, you don't want to be remembered as the graceless girl who could think of nothing but her own perceived misfortune. Even if you're going through a rough patch, it's no excuse to deny others their happiness. A selfless attitude now will reflect back on you in the future.

Excuse: You don't think you'll have a date to bring.

Why it's unacceptable: As a bridesmaid, you won't have much time to devote to a date, anyway. The dates of the wedding party, in fact, are often the most neglected and bored wedding guests at the party. Plus, going solo offers the opportunity to find a date for the next wedding you'll attend.

Excuse: You're pregnant.

Why it's unacceptable: If you are pregnant and dread donning the bridesmaid dress, think about your reasons for wanting out. Are you feeling self-conscious about looking bigger than the other bridesmaids? If so, talk to the bride about your concerns. The bride asked you to be a bridesmaid because she wants you by her side on her special day, so to bow out because you feel self-conscious may be something you regret down the line. If the wedding is very late in your pregnancy or you anticipate having health issues, explain your situation to the bride and ask if there is another way you can participate in her party.

Excuse: You're busy.

Why it's unacceptable: So is everyone else. Unless there is a specific conflict that goes above and beyond normal daily stress and obligations, simple busyness will not get you off the hook.

When all is said and done, this does not mean think of another, better excuse. Rather, if these are the reasons you do not want to be a bridesmaid, you should try your hardest to get over them. They are thoughts and feelings that have been shared by many a bridesmaid before you, but despite it all, they, too, survived—and became better friends in the process. Even if they seem good enough to you, rest assured they will be viewed as irrational and selfish by the bride and everyone she tells (in other words, all the other bridesmaids, her family, the groom's family, and half the wedding guests). So proceed only if you wish to risk being socially ostracized.

Bowing Out Gracefully

Even if every fiber of your being is crying out to take a walk down the aisle as a bridesmaid, there may simply be some obstacles preventing you from serving. If any of these scenarios describes your situation, remember: Don't decline before having a heart-to-heart chat with the bride. Perhaps your participation is important enough for her to be flexible about your level of commitment or responsibilities.

Excuse: You have very real financial concerns.

You, or your husband, have been laid off. You have unexpected medical or other bills. Or you are simply living on a shoestring budget. If your financial concerns are real—and you're not just cheaping out to avoid contributing to a shower—then even a few hundred dollars for a dress and preparties will really set you back. Talk to the bride, and explain your situation. She may already have an inkling of what's going on, or she may have no idea and appreciate your honesty. If she is a good friend, she obviously won't wish to burden you any further. She will either offer to help you with the expenses or will give you the option to decline with impunity.

Alert

Never lie or create false excuses for turning down a request to be a bridesmaid. Inevitably, you will be found out. At the very least, this is bad PR—you will suffer the long-term consequences of being known as a bad friend. Not to mention garnering a new place of honor on the bride's blacklist.

Excuse: You're geographically challenged.

If you simply can't be where you need to be at the appropriate time without some serious setbacks or major inconveniences, it will be difficult to serve as bridesmaid. You may be spending a semester abroad or living in a far-off city. Perhaps travel will be impossible due to your career, medical concerns, pregnancy, or very young children. The bride will understand if you can't reasonably get away—the key word being "reasonably."

Excuse: Other obligations won't permit it.

Perhaps you have a long-planned work trip you simply can't miss. Or the wedding is scheduled for the same day as your medical school graduation. Or maybe you've already agreed to be a bridesmaid in another wedding on the same day. Obviously, conflicts like these will prevent you from being a bridesmaid. Let the bride know as soon as possible about any suspected conflicts. If you are very close, the bride may even opt to change her wedding date so you'll be able to attend.

CHAPTER 2

The Maid of Honor

The maid of honor, aka the Alpha girl. The über-bridesmaid. The go-to gal. Before choking on too many metaphors, here's the upshot: The maid of honor is the bridesmaid in charge. If this is you, congratulations! You'll finally have a chance to show off those leadership skills you developed as sorority president or resident adviser in college. You will be the bride's confidant and right-hand gal. The bride is depending on you, so here's what you need to know.

The Ultimate Maid

Being asked to be the maid of honor is the ultimate compliment. This post implies not just that you're a good friend but also that you're a great organizer and that the bride can depend on you. Because beyond those reams of silk, satin, and pretty bows lies real work—the maid of honor is ultimately a role in which organization comes in much handier than aesthetics (though a sense of style, of course, never goes to waste).

Great Expectations

Being maid of honor will afford you much more responsibility than that of being bridesmaid. But before you begin stressing over the details, first take a moment to bask in the glory. Being someone's maid of honor is a true distinction, and you should feel proud and truly honored to have been asked.

 Fact

There is no difference between a maid of honor and a matron of honor other than marital status—matron indicates marriage. To date, there is no commonly used moniker for those seeking a marriage-neutral status, such as Ms. of honor, for instance.

Once you've finished patting yourself on the back, read ahead to find out how your duties differ. They will require a bit more effort than that of the rest of the bridesmaids. If you're a bit controlling by nature, you were born for this job—it's your chance to take charge without being questioned. If you're more comfortable as an enthusiastic follower, however, don't fret. The details in this chapter will walk you through all your duties, with ideas to make the job easier no matter what your style or leadership comfort level.

Ready to Help

Just so you don't forget or miss a thing, here is a basic list of typical maid of honor duties.

DUTIES OF THE MAID/MATRON OF HONOR:

- Helps the bride with addressing envelopes, recording wedding gifts, shopping, and other prewedding tasks
- Arranges a bridal shower
- Helps the bride arrange her train and veil at the altar
- Collects funds and organizes a group gift to the bride
- Brings the groom's ring to the ceremony, and holds it until the ring exchange
- Holds the bride's bouquet as she exchanges rings with the groom
- Signs the marriage certificate
- Stands in the receiving line (optional)
- Makes sure the bride looks perfect for all the pictures
- Dances with the best man during the attendants' dance at the reception
- Participates in the bouquet toss, if single
- Helps the bride change into getaway clothes

Co-Maid of Honoring

In some instances, the bride may just not be able to choose between her favorite ladies to be the maid of honor. Every lady in the wedding party holds a special place in her life, and she may decide that two maids of honor is the right choice for her. If this situation arises, don't feel slighted or hurt. The decision has (most likely) nothing to do with whether or not she thinks you can handle the job, but more about her bestowing this honor on two important people.

 **Essential**

> To keep things running smoothly between the two maids
> of honor, be sure to open the lines of communication with
> the other honor attendant right away, so that you avoid
> duplicating tasks and/or stepping on each other's toes.

Generally, the two maids of honor amicably split up the duties and work together well. Sometimes, the bride may step in and help divvy up the duties. There could be a number of reasons for having two maids of honor: One maid of honor may live out of town and not be able to assist with daily tasks; one maid of honor may have children, a demanding job, be in school, or have some other large obligation that does not allow her the time to devote to being the sole maid of honor; and often, brides will ask a younger sister, who is really too young to be planning bridal showers and bachelorette parties on her own, to be a maid of honor. Whatever the case, it is up to the maids of honor to work together to make the bride happy, even if they have differences.

Bridal Party Who's Who

As the organizer of the group, it is important that the maid of honor has all the contact information on the members of the bride's entourage, including addresses, home phone numbers, cell phone numbers, and e-mail addresses—possibly even their Twitter and Facebook accounts. It may also be helpful to have the contact information for the men in the party and the children. Keep all of your information organized and easy to find at a moment's notice with a roster of your wedding team. See the handy worksheets in the Appendix for help!

Essential

Being organized is the best skill you can have as maid of honor. Your first duty should be getting all the bridesmaids' pertinent contact information, including first and last names (if you don't already know them), phone numbers, e-mail addresses, and street addresses.

Planning with a Friend

While at first the idea of being a maid of honor may seem grand and exciting, and it certainly is, ultimately, this job is about the relationship you have with the bride. Yes, she has asked you to step up and be her right-hand gal. Yes, she may ask your opinion and want a true answer. But you must walk the fine line between maid of honor and friend. As you plan and assist your friend, you must always keep in mind that it is her experience, and coming out on the other end of it still friends is important.

Whether you're maid of honor or a bridesmaid, the bulk of your practical, time-intensive duties will come primarily during the engagement period, while the more ceremonial ones will take place on the wedding day itself. But unlike the bridesmaids, the maid of honor still carries some high-profile duties on the wedding day. But let's take first things first. What exactly are your responsibilities leading up to the wedding?

How to *Really* Help

Obviously, not every maid-of-honor experience is the same, and duties will differ based on the bride's preferences and requests. There are, however, some universal responsibilities you can expect to take on from the start. These range from leading the bridesmaids to planning parties to providing emotional support throughout the engagement. The level of each will depend on the bride, the style of wedding, and any other mitigating circumstances.

One of your main duties, and kind of what sums up the entire maid-of-honor position, is that you are the liaison between the bride and the bridesmaids. Being liaison entails communicating any pertinent information, such as:

- The dates and details of upcoming preparties
- Information on the bridesmaid attire
- The whats and whens of the wedding itself

The job of liaison also entails keeping the bridesmaids organized and on schedule with reminders and updates about things like fittings, dress pickups, and parties. This does not mean that the bride speaks only through you during the course of her engagement, but it does mean that she can count on you to impart any information to the greater mass of maids. If she's got a large number of bridesmaids, your role as information disseminator will be especially important, as the bride will find it much easier to tell one person—you—than to keep track of informing twelve people, while also balancing the rest of her wedding-planning tasks.

Managing the Troops

If the prospect of supervising and organizing a slew of bridesmaids that you may or may not know seems equally daunting to you, try adopting some of the following organizational strategies:

- Immediately get the properly spelled full names, e-mail addresses, and street addresses of all bridesmaids. Use the Bridesmaid Roster in the Appendix to organize this information.
- Set up a specific group e-mail list for bridesmaids on your computer—at home and at work.
- Set up a private (invitation-only) Facebook page.
- If there are more than ten bridesmaids, set up a telephone/e-mail/Twitter/Facebook chain in the event of an emergency or if information needs to get around quickly.
- Optional: Soon after the engagement is announced, host a get-together for all the bridesmaids to meet and greet (if they don't already know each other). This will break the ice, and is a fun prewedding activity for the bride. Plus, if you get to know them in person, it will be easier to plan parties, showers, and so on when the time comes.

Once you have your communication system set up, it will be easier to perform organizational tasks like directing the bridesmaids to order their dresses, letting them know when the dresses are ready to be fitted and altered, and advising them to pick them up in time for the wedding. In addition, you can ensure they have the rest of their attire ready, including shoes, jewelry, and the proper underwear (strapless bras, for instance). Obviously, they are adults who share the responsibility of getting what they need, on time, but it can't hurt to send them a few friendly little reminders (and, in fact, this is part of your official maid-of-honor duties).

The Bride's Liaison

Besides being the bride's liaison to the rest of the brides-maids, you will serve a dual role as the bride's personal ambassador to the world. Like a real-life ambassador, your duties will take on many and varied functions, depending on the daily circumstances. One day you may be asked to drop off color swatches at the florist; the next you may be called upon to mediate a conflict with the groom (i.e., listen while the bride vents). Because diplomacy may so often be called upon during the engagement period, your role as liaison can-not be underestimated, and it cannot be eclipsed by your other, more concrete duties, like planning the shower and bachelorette party.

Basically, the sketchy role of bride's liaison will require you to be a good friend. Even if the bride calls upon you to help with details that don't concern you or the bridesmaids directly (for example, the bride asks for help choosing the band or invita-tions), you should be ready and willing to lend a hand. The best maids of honor have been known to help scout out caterers and other vendors; help the bride shop for her wedding dress; assist in making wedding favors; help address invitations; and other-wise function as the bride's Gal Friday.

Obviously, there is potential for matters to get out of control—daily requests to run errands might prove a bit too demanding after a while. (You do have your own life to live, a fact occasion-ally forgotten by brides in the face of wedding planning.) But in general, be prepared to lend a hand when requested. If you're single, it's good practice for your own wedding; if you're married, it's a chance to lend the bride your hard-won expertise, and to relive the glory days of planning your own wedding.

Playing Hostess

If you don't have much experience hosting parties, as maid of honor you'll get it now . . . and fast! Two of your official and oh-so-important duties are to plan a shower and to plan a bachelorette party for the bride. While you can certainly solicit the help of other bridesmaids, the bride's mother, or other close friends or relatives, ultimately these events will reflect upon you.

🅔✔ Fact

The Internet can be a great source of help for party planning, with topics ranging from invitations to recipes to decorating tips. There are many sites devoted strictly to entertaining; just perform a quick search and they will pop up.

Luckily, there's help. If you don't have the first clue about what you're supposed to do, this chapter will help you narrow down your many options, as well as inform you, step by step, of what you need to do. And remember, it never hurts to ask for advice, and there are plenty of women who've gone before you who'd be willing to share it. Tap into the girl network for specific recommendations on caterers, punch recipes, games, or activities—you never know what gems you'll come up with.

Shower Her with Attention

One of the most substantial duties you will have as maid of honor is to plan and coordinate a shower for the bride. This may be a task you choose to take on yourself, or you may decide to enlist the aid of the bridesmaids (financial and organizational).

It's entirely up to you, and you should make your intentions clear—the bridesmaids will look to you to get the ball rolling with the shower plans.

Bridal showers generally involve a pattern of serving refreshments, followed by gift giving, interspersed with party games. The level to which you take each of these is entirely dependent on your preferences (and the bride's), and will vary depending upon your budget and entertaining style. For example, you may wish to host a shower in a restaurant, or you may want to keep things simpler and have it at home, serving just cake and punch.

🅔 Alert

When planning a shower, choose an option that suits your lifestyle. While a shower in a restaurant may seem easy and elegant, it's also going to be a lot more expensive than hosting a party at home. However, if you just don't have the time or resources to throw a party at home, a restaurant may be just the ticket.

Celebrating the Bachelorette

You've got this shower thing under control with great style and success, and just when you thought you were off the hook, there's one more event to consider—the bachelorette party. This party should be a little easier to plan, as it involves activities you probably do more regularly—a night on the town, for example, or a day at a spa.

The Girls' Answer to Bachelor Parties

The bachelorette party basically developed as a response to the boys' long-revered bachelor party, and it is a relatively recent phenomenon among the girls—after all, why should boys have all the fun? Of course, the bachelorette party that you plan doesn't need to be as raucous as the typical bachelor party . . . but then again, it can be if that's what the bride wants.

🅔! Alert

There's only one way to decide what tone the bachelorette party should take, and that is to check with the bride. It is even more crucial with this party than with the shower festivities.

You should already have a pretty clear indication of the bride's likes and dislikes when it comes to a night of revelry with the girls. Based on her personality and regular activities, you probably already have some idea of whether she'd like a wild night of barhopping or a more subdued spa weekend. If she's not into the bar scene, plunging her into a night of clubhopping and male strippers may make her uncomfortable. On the other hand, even the most mild-mannered gal may wish to seize this opportunity to let it all hang out while she's still a swinging single. The moral of this story is, ask!

Details and Duties

As a maid of honor, you will be part of a whirlwind of fun, excitement, planning, and parties. At times it may seem a little crazy, at times it will be stressful, but hopefully most of the time you will think it is a fun and joyous experience. Here is a little primer on what details and duties may come your way as you go down the maid of honor road.

The Hunt for the Dress

As you may or may not already know, another of the maid of honor's duties is to help shop for the bridesmaid dress and accessories. You'll face one of two scenarios: a bride who knows exactly what color and style dress she wants her maids to wear, or a bride who has no clue and seeks your expert input. If your bride falls into the former category, you hope she's chosen a style that's tremendously flattering, or else you're out of luck. If she falls into the latter, you are very fortunate, as you'll have a strong say in what you'll be wearing on the big day. This is a great opportunity to steer the bride toward a style you like and can afford. Seize it, and make the most of it.

One Size Does Not Fit All

When helping the bride choose bridesmaid dresses, consider the interests of all the bridesmaids. That means avoiding too-revealing or too-sexy styles . . . even if they'd happen to look perfect on you. Remember, this dress is not just for you. Even though you may be a perfectly proportioned size four, chances are there will be some variation in size among the remaining bridesmaids.

As tempting as it may be to choose the red spaghetti-strap number with the plunging neckline, bridesmaids who are, say, particularly large-chested or very small-chested may not feel quite as comfortable in it as you. Nor will most bridesmaids above a size two feel comfortable wearing a mermaid-style sheath. The bottom line? Be sensitive to everyone's comfort, not just your own.

Of course, another option is that the maid of honor dresses differently than the rest of the bridesmaids. This may entail wearing a dress of the same color in a slightly different style or wearing the same dress with an added accent piece, such as a wrap or special adornment. It's been a popular trend in recent years for the maid of honor to stand out in some way from the rest of the bridesmaids, in which case you'll really be free to choose a dress that's flattering to you.

Fact

The maid of honor and the rest of the bridesmaids are responsible for footing the full cost of their bridesmaid attire and accessories, including shoes, hosiery, and specialty undergarments.

Of course, the financial responsibility for the dress, shoes, accessories, and jewelry ultimately lies with you. Occasionally, a bride has been known to subsidize or pay for her bridesmaids' dresses, but she is rare indeed; definitely set a few bucks aside and expect to pay the full amount for all your attire, and don't forget about special underwear needs, such as hosiery, special bras, or other support wear.

Party Guest Extraordinaire

The maid of honor is to attend all prewedding parties, including engagement parties, showers, the bachelorette party (or parties), the bridesmaids' luncheon, and the rehearsal dinner. Obviously, if you live far away, it will prove a challenge to attend every prewedding gathering. Unless you're dealing with a really high-maintenance bride, she will hardly expect you to drop everything and fly in repeatedly prior to the wedding.

If the thought of being party guest extraordinaire is leaving you exhausted or drained, pick and choose the events you'll be able to attend . . . but ask the bride which events she would prefer you to attend. For example, if there are two engagement parties, try to get to at least one, and talk to the bride about which one she'd prefer you attend. Also, talk to the bride about potentially consolidating events into one weekend or single timeframe—have the shower the same weekend as the bachelorette party, for example, or have multiple events in the week leading up to the wedding.

 **Essential**

As the maid of honor, you can exert some of your influence in planning her shower to be the same weekend as another event. This will help other out-of-town bridesmaids or guests attend as many events as possible.

Playing the Part

So what is your role at these parties, anyway? Simply put, as maid of honor, you will be the bride's right-hand gal. Here is more of what's expected of you:

- At the engagement party, you want to meet all the people you'll be dealing with over the next few months, including the groomsmen and the groom's close family and friends (presuming you already know the bride's family). You should also take this early opportunity to get to know any bridesmaids you haven't already met. If you're a college friend of the bride's, for instance, it's possible you've never met her high school friends.
- At the showers, you will be in charge of tracking all the bride's gifts by keeping copious notes on who gave what. (You may also delegate this task to one of the other bridesmaids if you're busy helping in some other

capacity, like hosting.) This record keeping will help the bride after the shower, when she writes thank-you notes for all the gifts she's received. Be sure that you or the bridesmaid handling this task writes down a description of each gift in detail, along with the corresponding gift giver. In all the excitement, the bride will be hard pressed to remember these details later, especially if it's a large shower or she's had more than one.

- You will also probably host (or cohost) one of the bride's showers.
- At the bridesmaids' luncheon, you are simply there to enjoy yourself. This event is hosted by the bride in appreciation of the bridal party's help over the course of the engagement.
- At the rehearsal dinner, you can make yourself especially useful by helping organize everyone for the wedding day. You might make sure the key players have transportation for the wedding day; reconfirm wedding-day beauty appointments for the bridesmaids; and ensure all the men know what time they're supposed to show up at the chapel.

Fact

At all the wedding preparties, including engagement parties, showers, the bachelorette party, and the rehearsal dinner, the maid of honor should make herself available and accessible to help the bride and her mother wherever needed.

Wedding Day Duties

So you've completed all your prewedding-day duties with great style and success. After all this planning and prepartying, you can hardly believe the main event hasn't happened yet. But here it is, and your responsibilities continue. After all, this is what you've all been working up to.

 Essential

> It's a good idea to include transportation on your itinerary—how each girl is getting to each place. This will keep Bridesmaid No. 2 from driving off and leaving you—or the bride!—stranded at the hair salon.

The wedding day can be very tense and stressful for the bride, and you, lucky girl, can make it much easier for her. From the moment you wake up, your job will be to attend to the bride's needs and concerns. Some brides may not want anything from you except to enjoy your company, while others may have you running around like a feline on catnip. The more organized the bride has been, the less you'll probably have to do—pending any unexpected circumstances like weather, no-show vendors, or other wedding-related disasters.

The Morning of the Wedding

If the wedding is in the afternoon, most likely you, the bride, and the bridesmaids are planning to use the hours leading up to the ceremony to get ready. This may involve appointments at the salon, massages, and manicures and/or pedicures—a veritable beauty bonanza.

As maid of honor, you should have everyone's schedules written down to refer to, especially if you, the bride, or the bridesmaids have multiple appointments. This way you can serve as the go-to girl for the bridesmaids and the salon and spa that you're visiting. To be sure everyone knows where to be and when, you may consider giving each bridesmaid her own written wedding-day itinerary at the rehearsal dinner. This is a particularly helpful strategy if there are lots of activities and appointments you'll need to keep track of on the day of the wedding.

Once you're all ready and beautiful, your next job is to organize the bridesmaids' bouquets when they arrive from the florist. Sort them out and confirm that each bridesmaid has her own bouquet, and that none have been forgotten. If there is any problem with the flowers, troubleshoot with the florist on the bride's behalf.

Many brides choose to have as many photographs as possible taken before the wedding ceremony. You may wish to suggest she set aside forty-five minutes to an hour before the wedding to take pictures with her parents and the bridesmaids, cutting some of the postwedding photo time you'll need. Plus, you'll all be looking your freshest and best before the day's many activities begin.

If you need to, help organize the progression of photos throughout the wedding day. For example, the bride may wish to have formal portraits taken with her parents, you, all the bridesmaids, and her flower girls, separately as well as together. Advise her to give a written list to the photographer to ensure none of these are forgotten. Then, be sure to offer your assistance to the photographer when it is time to find the key players.

The Ceremony

The maid of honor's most important ceremonial duties involve keeping the bride looking good and feeling organized. These duties begin the moment you arrive at the ceremony site. As soon as you get there, take a moment to rearrange the bride's dress, train, veil, hair, and makeup, if necessary. Oftentimes, the car ride can result in a bunched-up train or wind can mess that perfectly coiffed 'do.

CEREMONY RESPONSIBILITIES

- Walking down the aisle, immediately preceding the bride.
- Artfully arranging the bride's dress, train, and veil when she reaches the end of the aisle. You'll want to help her ensure that her dress looks perfectly arranged for photographs. If it's an especially long train, you may wish to have another bridesmaid help you lay it out behind her.
- Holding on to the groom's ring and giving it to the bride at the appropriate time during the ceremony. Be sure to keep it in a very safe place—such as your thumb—so you won't lose it or forget to carry it down the aisle.
- Holding the bride's bouquet during the ceremony. This means placing your bouquet on a chair or church pew and holding hers so the flowers don't get crushed or bent.
- Acting as a formal witness to the marriage. This involves signing the marriage license and any religious documents that may be included in the formal wedding ceremony.

After the Wedding Ceremony

Congratulations! You've done your duty. The bride is successfully married and looking her best. But just when you thought your wedding-day tasks were done, don't go anywhere quite yet . . . there's more.

Your first responsibility immediately follows the wedding ceremony, and it includes participating in the receiving line. This is when the bride, groom, their parents, and sometimes the honor attendants (maid of honor and best man) stand and greet all the guests who've come to the wedding ceremony. The bride may ask that you participate in the receiving line, or she may prefer you mingle among the guests—it's up to her whether you'll be part of the line itself.

Essential

Obviously, you will be the subject of many photographs during the ceremony, as well. As if there's not enough to think about, don't forget to make an effort to stand up straight and keep a neutral expression or smile on your face, or be ready to get caught on film with some unflattering looks.

If you are a part of the receiving line, your only tasks may be to simply stand there and smile. No one really knows what to say in the ten to twenty seconds allotted to each receiving-line exchange (and chances are that many of these exchanges will involve virtual strangers), so think of a few throwaway lines beforehand like "Great to see you," "Beautiful dress," or "Gorgeous day" to keep the guests occupied with small talk, should they falter.

Winding Down Your Duties

If the reception is at a different location than the ceremony, you'll want to help the bride freshen up as soon as you arrive.

That means assisting her with any touchups to makeup, hair, dress or veil, and bustling her dress if necessary (bustling is usually quite simple—there are loops/ties that correspond to buttons/ties on the dress).

Essential

It is inevitable that the bride will have to use the bathroom—and this will definitely require your help. Be prepared! You will also be called upon to help rearrange stockings and underwear once she's done . . . all in the name of friendship.

There is also a public role you, the maid of honor, will need to fulfill at the reception. This includes general hosting, dancing with the best man (if there is a wedding-party dance), and collecting any wedding-gift envelopes from guests. The bride will probably have a designated envelope collector—her father, the best man, or maybe you—to consolidate these envelopes as they are offered. If you are the one assigned this task, be extremely careful about keeping track of them—most will contain checks or even cash gifts.

Let the Good Times Roll

Ahhhh, the reception. You can let loose, find your date, and forget about responsibility for the rest of the night, now, right? Wrong! This gig isn't over until the bride manages to get out of her dress (that's right, you may even have to help her there). Throughout the evening, it is the maid of honor's duty to attend to the bride as well as act as a hostess of sorts to the guests. You also may be called upon to make a toast.

For many years, tradition has held that the best man gives a speech before the meal. But as with the bachelor party, why should the boys have all the fun? In recent years, it's become increasingly common to hear a toast from the maid of honor as well as the best man. And why not? You've got as much to say as the best man.

🅔❗ Alert

If you dread speaking in public, you've got no obligation to give a toast to the happy couple. Consult the bride's favorite book of poems or favorite songs for help. If all else fails, it's your prerogative to keep your lips zipped.

If you do plan to say a few words, let the bride, groom, and best man know in advance, so they can pass the mic to you at the appropriate time. This could be either before or after the best man's toast. But what should you say? Well, that's entirely up to you. Tell a funny anecdote about the bride and groom or a sentimental story about the bride and her family.

TOASTING TIPS

- Brainstorm ideas to develop your theme. Consider how the bride and groom met, the first time you met the groom, your history with the bride and her family, or events that emerged during the engagement. Your toast/ speech can be funny or touching—say what feels most natural and appropriate for this wedding.
- Consider whether you'd like to precede or follow the best man's speech with your own. Do you want the audience warmed up beforehand, or would you rather dazzle them right off the bat?

- Consider your audience. This is a diverse group, probably ranging in age from eight to eighty. Try to appeal to every guest with universal themes, references, and speech patterns. Avoid slang terms and repeated use of phrases including "like," "you know," and "um."
- Start with a catchy opening. It can be a joke or a quick anecdote, but it should capture the attention of the guests right away.
- Maintain eye contact. Don't stare at your cue cards or at the table. Try to keep your gaze focused on various guests around the room. (But consult cards if you need to.)
- Take a few deep breaths before you begin your speech, stand up straight, and project your voice.
- Practice, practice, practice! Rehearse your speech in front of a mirror or consult a trusted friend for an honest opinion. There's no better way to get it just right at the wedding.
- Never include off-color jokes, racy stories, or confidential information in your speech. Keep the subject matter positive and upbeat.
- Keep your toast brief, just a few minutes long. Too long-winded, and you'll lose the attention of your audience, especially if yours is just one of many toasts/speeches.

Post Hoopla

As the wedding festivities come to a close, the maid of honor plays a crucial role. After enjoying a wonderful day, the last thing a bride needs to do is pack her bags, gather her things, and worry about how her bouquet is getting to the preservationist or the rentals back to the rental company. Here is a brief list of how to help the bride one last time:

- Gather her things from the bridal room. Pack them and get them into the limousine or car that will take them to their wedding-night accommodations.
- Assist the bride in changing into her going-away outfit, and possibly even be responsible for the wedding dress.
- Take the bride's bouquet from her and get it on its way to the bouquet preservationist (which the bride should have prearranged).
- Gather small rental items that need to be returned, or oversee the rental company pick up.
- Pack up personal items such as the guest book, toasting glasses, and cake server and take them home with you.
- Take the top tier of the cake home, wrap it up tightly in plastic wrap and foil (or a freezer-safe container), and store it in the freezer.

CHAPTER 3

Chatting about Cash

The first question on any bridesmaid's mind is usually—and understandably—one of finances. Unfortunately, while most brides do try to be cost conscious, you may encounter the exception to that rule—the bride to whom money is no object when it comes to her dream day . . . and who assumes everyone else feels the same way. What to do? What to say? How much is this going to cost? This chapter covers a variety of contingencies, and offers up some money-saving tips for bridesmaids who care to save a buck or two.

What's the Bottom Line?

If you have served as a bridesmaid for multiple weddings, you'll see they have one thing in common—each is different. Every wedding and bridesmaid experience varies based on all the details of that particular wedding, including the wedding's location, the level of formality, the style of dress, and any other special requests that the bride makes. Overwhelmed? Confused? Well, help is on the way. A little guidance and introduction to average expenses for some of the more common nuptial scenarios will help get you on your way.

 Alert

Understanding the financial responsibilities of the wedding from the outset will help you budget properly. Where possible, avoid using credit cards, as you'll pay a whopping interest rate that will overinflate your expenses. (For instance, that $200 bridesmaid dress will end up costing you $300 once the interest has compounded.)

Expenses, Expenses

Yes, you are going to hear it again: each wedding, each bride is different. However, it never hurts to know what you could be in for. Here is a checklist of typical costs you may incur as a member of the wedding party.

The bride's attendants pay for:

- Their dresses and accessories
- A shower gift
- Part of the bridal shower and bachelorette party

- Transportation to and from the wedding
- A gift for the couple

Now, that is the simplified version of costs. When it really comes down to it, there are many more times you'll be pulling out your wallet, and much of it depends on the scale of the wedding the bride is planning. Further on in this section, you will see some additional expense breakdowns based on the style and logistics of different weddings.

Cost-Cutting Measures

No matter what the style of wedding—destination, theme, or otherwise—there are still some strategies you can use to cut the estimated costs. These strategies are meant to achieve the same—or virtually the same—results, but at a lower cost. In other words, do not boycott the bride's choice of dress or defy the bride's wishes for a special up-do (as unreasonable as that may feel to you). The following strategies are simply meant to help you cut corners in the areas where you'll be likely to get away with it.

The Bridesmaid Attire

The bridesmaid dress is the bridesmaid dress. Once the bride has chosen it, there's little any of the bridesmaids can do about it. You can Facebook it or tweet it, but hold off announcing your displeasure publicly! There's little you'll be able to do to cut this expense. However, you may be able to cut some of the ancillary attire costs, including the following:

Alterations

Many times a bridal salon or dress shop, like most wedding vendors, will charge you more than the competitive market rate for alterations; many times an independent tailor or seamstress will charge significantly less. If you already know a trusted seamstress, bring the dress to her for any hemming or alterations. If you don't know of anyone offhand, ask for recommendations from the other bridesmaids, family members, or friends, or even your regular dry cleaner.

 Fact

Most bridesmaid dresses are cut on the smallish side, so don't worry if you end up ordering them a size (or two or three) larger than your regular size. Carefully follow the salon's guidelines for taking your measurements. It's a lot easier (and cheaper) to tailor a dress down than it is to make it larger.

Shoes

If the bride hasn't specified her choice in shoes, ask if you can wear a pair you already own. If she has her heart set on dyeables, see if she'll agree to purchasing them at a less expensive store like Payless, which often charges half what other shoe stores do. Or ask if she'd mind if you dye a pair that you already own in a color to match the dress. (Obviously, the store won't be able to dye a pair of emerald green shoes pink; use your judgment here.)

Accessories

If the bride doesn't offer accessories as a gift and she doesn't specify a preference in what accessories you wear, then you have options. You can go for a simple look, with little to no jewelry; you might try wearing a classic piece you already own, such as a strand of pearls; you can raid your mother's or sister's jewelry box for a fun piece; or you can buy something new, on sale, at a costume jewelry shop or department store. If you do buy something, the key is picking a piece you'll wear again and again, not just with your bridesmaid dress.

ⓔ✔ Fact

Often the bride will give attendants necklaces and/or earrings or an evening bag as a special gift before the wedding so the bridesmaids are all wearing the same accessories.

Hair and Makeup

If the bride wishes to schedule group appointments for professionally coiffed hair or makeup application on the morning of the wedding, find out in advance what the salon will charge for each service. If you can't afford it, opt out (if the bride has given you a choice), and meet up with the group afterward. You can do your own hair and makeup, go to a salon that you know will charge less, or have a talented friend or sister do the honors.

Travel Costs

If you're traveling to your wedding destination, flying will most likely be the biggest travel-related expense. The first thing you may want to consider is driving to your destination, if possible. If you're used to flying, it might be an inconvenience, but it could also save you a lot of money. For instance, when you weigh the cost of a flight for two people from Buffalo to Philadelphia, the savings could be well worth the seven-hour drive. Plus, if you drive, you'll save on the cost of a rental car once you get there—as good as another few hundred dollars in your pocket.

If you do decide to fly or have little choice, based on the distance of your destination, consider alternate destinations served by lower-cost airlines. For instance, if you're flying to Washington, DC, you may consider flying into Baltimore/Washington International instead of Dulles or Reagan National Airport to take advantage of cheaper flights offered by discount airlines like Southwest. It may be a little farther from your final destination, but it could also save you hundreds of dollars.

🔵 Essential

Try using discount travel websites to find low fares. Some lower-cost airlines are not included on these sites, so be sure to check their websites for lower fares before booking. Also, don't rule out package deals and cost savers.

You should also consider strategies that include things like flying on less popular, thus less expensive, days like Saturday and Tuesday, and making your reservations well in advance. Also consider using frequent flyer miles or redeeming credit card points for free or less expensive airline tickets.

If you do fly, you'll need some way to get around once you get there. If you decide to rent a car, see if any of the other bridesmaids would like to share the rental; after all, you'll be running around doing the same things all weekend anyway. Public transportation may be a more practical solution, especially if you're staying in a city like New York, where a rental car can be more of a hindrance than a help.

Affordable Accommodations

If the wedding is out of town, chances are the bride or groom's family has sent information on recommended accommodations. Often, they've already negotiated a discount rate at a hotel based upon the volume of guests the wedding will guarantee, so this may be your lowest rate for the area. But if it still seems high, feel free to do some detective work on other nearby hotels, bed-and-breakfasts, or motels. You may discover accommodations that suit your budget much better.

Question

How else could I save on accommodations?
You may also wish to double up with a friend or a bridesmaid to cut the cost of your hotel room in half. You'll inevitably spend little time in your hotel room anyway, with all the activities and responsibilities the weekend will bring.

Obviously, the least expensive accommodations are with friends or family. Get the word out that you'll be in town, and hope you'll be extended an invitation. If you get one, be sure to bring a hostess gift (flowers, candy, baked goods—any thoughtful small gift will do) and be considerate during your stay. And don't forget to send a thank-you note after you get home!

Low-Priced Parties

Who ever said a good party has to be expensive? The success of a party ultimately depends on the guest list and a good vibe; whether you're drinking beer or champagne shouldn't make much of a difference.

Ultimately, how and where you throw a shower and bachelorette party is not solely your decision. The maid of honor generally spearheads this process, with financial and organizational help from the bridesmaids. That means you should all get together in person, by phone, or via e-mail to begin deciding the best course of action. See the next section in this chapter regarding the nuts and bolts of shower planning.

With that said, there are certain money-saving strategies you can adopt while planning the shower. A shower at someone's home will be much less expensive than a restaurant or country club shower, for instance, and a shower with snacks and refreshments only will be easier on the budget than serving a full meal.

Essential

The amount you spend on a gift is not important; rather, it's the thought and ability behind the gift you're giving that should be valued. Of course, that's easier said than believed. But remember, they are offerings of goodwill, not obligations.

A home-based bachelorette party can be much less expensive than a night on the town as well, and no less fun. Read on for specific ideas on creative bachelorette parties you can have at home, along with ideas for a fun evening out.

Gifts in Good Taste

Now, you may be wondering, with all of these other expenses, are you still required to give a shower and a wedding gift? Technically, a wedding gift is a voluntary offering, a sign of celebration and support of the marriage, but not required. That being said, there are few guests who would forego purchasing a wedding gift for the couple. On the other hand, a shower gift is expected, as that is the purpose of a bridal shower. As a bridesmaid it is appropriate to give a gift for both the shower and the wedding. You'll surely feel awkward if you're the only bridesmaid who opts not to.

If you're strapped for cash after all these other expenses, you do have some options. Do you have a special talent, like photography, painting, or sewing? Give a homemade gift like a framed or mounted photo, an original watercolor, or an embroidered pillow. Only the most hardhearted of brides wouldn't love a gift that's so personal and unique.

Which Way Will She Wed?

The style and scale of the wedding the bride is planning will have the most affect on your bottom line. It is her wedding, after all, and she has a vision. How does your budget fit into her vision? How does your budget adapt to her style? Now is the time to find out and figure out what it takes to be a bridesmaid in a wedding.

The Budget-Conscious Wedding

So your bride's always been thrifty? Then maybe she'll exploit her budget-conscious nature in deference to her bridesmaids, too, though you shouldn't count on past thriftiness to be an indication of wedding costs—some of the biggest penny pinchers know no boundaries for their own weddings.

There is always the possibility that the bride is just extra considerate of the financial constraints of her closest friends and family members. Regardless, this bride is working hard to keep costs down, and she will, at the very least, give you options. For example, she'll tell you that a trip to the salon for wedding-day hair and makeup is optional or the black strappy sandals you already own are perfectly fine to wear. Thus, your expenses can end up being dramatically lower than many of the earlier scenarios.

One exception to expenses is the cost of travel. If you've got to travel, there's not much the bride can do, short of covering your expenses, which you should not count on. However, she may seek out free accommodations for you among family or friends.

Basic Budget-Conscious Wedding Costs	
Dress:	$75–$150
Alterations:	$30–$60
Shoes:	$0–$50
Accessories/jewelry:	$0–$20
Hair and makeup:	$0–$150
Shower:	$150 (shared expense)
Bachelorette party:	$100 (shared expense)
Shower gift:	$40
Wedding gift:	$100
Shower travel costs:	$0 (We'll assume it's in your hometown.)
Wedding travel costs and accommodations:	$0 (We'll assume it's in your hometown.)
Additional travel costs (tipping, room service, etc.):	$0
Total:	Starting at $495+ (tack on $1,000+ for travel if the wedding is out of town)

Obviously, the budget-conscious bride can keep costs much lower than the average by allowing you to wear your own shoes (or buy them cheaply), wear your own accessories or by purchasing them for you as bridal party gifts, and by not demanding professional hair and makeup services. She'll also make an effort to choose a less expensive dress, maybe even an off-the-rack dress from a department store or specialty store. All of these strategies will cut costs significantly, as well as allow the bridesmaids to exhibit some of their own personal style.

The Designer Wedding

So, you have a friend in your life who is very cool, very stylish, and very, well, loaded. Now she's asked you to be her bridesmaid, which is great, except that while she's been shopping Prada, you've been perusing Target. You can only imagine the dent in your pocketbook that the designer bridesmaid dress, fabulous shoes, and accessories she is going to choose for her attendants will make.

❶ Alert

Just because the bride has expensive tastes doesn't mean you need to buy an extravagant wedding gift. You should always give only what you can afford, and you can choose something elegant and tasteful in any price range.

You hope she'll realize quickly that not all of her bridesmaids are capable of spending like her and that she will make her choices accordingly. However, chances are she still won't be choosing the cheapest meal on the menu, and unfortunately, you'll still have to swallow it. You may also face some slightly higher shower and bachelorette party costs, particularly if the majority of the other bridesmaids (or the maid of honor) share her lifestyle. So what will that mean? An increase on the average prices of all your attire, from head to toe, plus parties.

Costs for a Designer Wedding	
Dress:	$300–$500
Alterations:	$75–$125
Shoes:	$100–$400
Accessories/jewelry:	$75–$200
Hair and makeup:	$150–$300
Shower:	$350 (shared expense)
Bachelorette party:	$100–$1,500 ($1,500?! Yes, if the party's in Vegas. Shared expense.)
Shower gift:	$50–75
Wedding gift:	$100–$200
Shower travel costs:	$0 (We'll assume it's in your hometown.)
Wedding travel costs:	$0
Accommodations:	$0
Additional travel costs:	$0 (tipping, room service, etc.):
Total:	**Starting at $1,300+ (add in an extra $1,000+ if the wedding is out of town)**

In-Town Hoopla

So, you're lucky enough to be serving a bride with a wedding locale close to home. Being in close proximity makes everything easier, from organizing parties to paying for expenses. Plus, responsibilities like dress fittings won't take on Herculean logistical proportions as you attempt to time the dress's arrival with the shower (so you can pick it up while you're in the bride's hometown), along with scheduling enough time before the wedding for alterations. (Of course, many shops will deliver your dress, too, for a cost. Expect to pay around $25–$50 if the dresses are purchased at a shop but shipped to your home.)

Costs for the In-Town Wedding	
Dress:	$150–$400
Alterations:	$50–$100
Shoes:	$50–$100
Accessories/jewelry:	$50–$75
Hair and makeup:	$100–$200
Shower:	$200 (shared expense)
Bachelorette party:	$150
Shower gift:	$40
Wedding gift:	$100–$200
Shower travel costs:	$0
Wedding travel costs:	$0
Hotel costs (wedding):	$0 per night
Additional travel costs:	$0 (tipping, room service, etc.):
Total:	**starting at $890+ (a significant savings from the out-of-town wedding)**

New Ways to Bridesmaid

Now that the more common "ways to bridesmaid" have been covered, let's chat about the new ways brides are choosing to wed and what that means for the bridesmaids. As brides get more creative and adventurous in their planning, there are new expectations and new expenses that a bridesmaid needs to be on the lookout for.

The Out-of-Town Affair

You're a lady of the world. You left town for college, traveled abroad, and moved to an exciting new city—or two—after you graduated. You've got close friends in every port, from every stage of your life: grammar school, high school, summer camp, college, graduate school, and your working years. Not to mention family members who've also moved around to different areas of the country or the world.

Inevitably, that means you'll be attending weddings all over the country and possibly even the world! What's more fun than discovering a new place, or rediscovering an old one? Of course, with the good sometimes comes the challenging, because travel inevitably means additional expenses. But hey, it's for a good cause and a good friend. If you're a bridesmaid, that may even mean multiple trips to the city/town of choice— one for the wedding and one or two additional trips for the showers, bachelorette party, or engagement party. If it's a far-away destination, obviously, the expenses can add up quickly.

Costs for an Out-of-Town Wedding	
Dress:	$150–$400
Alterations:	$50–$100
Shoes:	$50–$100
Accessories/jewelry:	$50–$75
Hair and makeup:	$100–$200
Shower:	$250 (shared expense)
Bachelorette party:	$100 (shared expense)
Shower gift:	$40–$70
Wedding gift:	$100–$200
Shower travel costs:	$300–$700
Wedding travel costs:	$300–$700 (Double that if you're bringing a date/husband.)
Hotel costs (wedding):	$100–$200 per night
Additional travel costs:	$100–$200 (tipping, room service, and so on)
Total:	**Starting at $1,690+ ($3,290+ including date/spouse)**

The Theme Wedding

There is always the chance that the bride has decided to plan a theme wedding. Not theme as in pink roses and lace, but a theme that will definitely need specialized attire and accessorizing for pulling it off, such as medieval or Victorian. Finding the appropriate outfit and achieving the look is what will make this wedding stand out from traditional, nonthematic weddings. This unique look is the factor that can translate into unique costs, as well.

🅔✔ Fact

If you are married or are bringing a date and it is requested the guest come in appropriate or thematic costume, expect your attire costs to double. It is just what is appropriate.

The problem with estimating these costs, however, is that they are extremely difficult to predict, especially with variations in the extravagance and availability of costumes for certain themes. However, the following provides a rough estimate for the bridesmaid participating in a theme wedding:

Costs for a Theme Wedding	
Dress/Attire:	$100–$400 (A rental costume may fall on the lower end of the cost spectrum, while purchasing that great vintage dress will raise it.)
Alterations:	$50-$100
Shoes:	$50-$100
Accessories/jewelry:	$50-$100
Hair and makeup:	$125–$250

Costs for a Theme Wedding	
Shower:	$200 (shared expense)
Bachelorette party:	$100–$150 (shared expense)
Shower gift:	$40–$80
Wedding gift:	$100–$200
Shower travel costs:	$300–$700 (If necessary; theme does not necessarily translate into travel)
Wedding travel costs:	$300–$700 (If necessary; theme does not necessarily translate into travel. Double that if you're bringing a date/husband.)
Hotel costs (wedding):	$100–$350 per night
Additional travel costs:	$50 (tipping, room service, etc.)
Total:	**Starting at $1,545+ (Included are travel costs, in the event this wedding is also out of town.)**

As you can see, the most significant variation you'll find when dealing with a theme wedding is in the cost of your bridesmaid's attire. This may be a good thing or a bad thing. If the bride is planning a Renaissance wedding, for example, you may end up spending less than you would on a traditional bridesmaid's dress if, for example, you'll be renting an outfit from a costume shop (expect to pay $100–$200).

Consequently, if the bride is throwing an over-the-top fairy-tale princess wedding, you may be saddled with additional costs for more extravagant bridesmaid dresses, tiaras, special shoes, and other jewelry you might not otherwise have required. Or, if she's throwing a funky disco wedding, you may feel compelled to buy that vintage Halston dress that you just know saw the likes of Studio 54 and needs to be put back into the circuit. So, as you've probably ascertained, a theme wedding is a bit more difficult to predict, as the attire can range dramatically from one theme wedding to the next.

Fact

A theme wedding incorporates an unusual, creative element into the wedding tradition. Popular themes include medieval weddings and Cinderella weddings, whereas more unusual themes may include underwater weddings or hot-air balloon celebrations.

On another note, either the bride may expect or you may be inspired to throw a shower or bachelorette party that coordinates with the wedding theme. This would probably add to the bottom line of the shower and bachelorette party. Incorporating a theme into either of these parties has the potential for additional expenses like a special location (the grounds of a medieval fair, for instance) or for decorations that will reflect the theme (disco ball, multitiered dance floor). Obviously, though, this will ultimately be up to you and the rest of the bridesmaids to decide on and budget for.

The Destination Wedding

There's a difference between destination weddings and out-of-town weddings. Destination weddings are almost mini-vacations and will typically send you off to a unique, exotic locale; an out-of-town wedding may simply send you back to your hometown or to the hometown of the bride. The popularity of destination weddings has grown in recent years, and couples that hold them typically want a wedding that's a bit more intimate or way off the beaten track.

So what does the destination wedding mean for you? A number of things. You'll be traveling somewhere you may have never been before, and you'll probably be staying longer than you would for a traditional weekend wedding. This translates, obviously, into higher costs. There is one exception: if the bride and groom (or their families) are paying the travel and accommodation costs. If it's a very small group that's attending, the wedding couple may use the funds they would have spent on a 300-guest wedding for the travel and hotel costs of the group they've invited. But don't assume or expect this. Obviously, travel and accommodation costs for a group of even ten people can add up quickly.

ⓔ✱ Essential

While destination weddings are usually smaller and more intimate—including just close family and friends—there are exceptions to every rule. Some destination weddings are simply traditional weddings, transplanted to a more exotic locale.

So what can you expect? Let's assume the wedding will be held at an all-inclusive resort in the Caribbean—a very popular location for destination weddings. The wedding couple, their family, and their friends are invited to spend the five days leading up to the wedding at the resort; the fifth day will culminate with the wedding. How much will this cost?

Costs for a Destination Wedding	
Dress:	$200–$350
Alterations:	$50
Shoes:	$0 (it's a barefoot-on-the-beach wedding) to $100

Costs for a Destination Wedding	
Accessories/jewelry:	$50
Hair and makeup:	$125–$175
Shower:	$200 (shared expense)
Bachelorette party:	$100–$200 (shared expense)
Shower gift:	$40–$100
Wedding gift:	$100–$200
Shower travel costs:	$0 (We'll assume it was in your hometown.)
Wedding travel costs:	$1,500–$2,500 (airfare and accommodations; double that if you're bringing a date/husband)
Additional travel costs:	$50 (tipping, room service, etc.):
Total:	**Starting at $2,365+**

Fashion File

Luckily, the days of awful bridesmaid dresses with flounces, bows, and fabric in all the wrong places are virtually over, as many designers have jumped on the opportunity to create chic and largely flattering dresses that reflect current trends and tastes. The bad rap does still remain to some extent—some brides have a lapse in judgment when it comes to bridesmaids dresses, no matter how good their taste and style is otherwise.

One Size Fits All?

Finding a dress that will look good on six completely different women is a task all in itself! Fortunately, dress designers have realized this fact as well, and current trends are reflecting the inevitable fact that all women will not fit well in the same dress. Thus, bridesmaid fashion's most current trend is the rise of the two-piece dress. These dresses typically feature tops and bottoms that can be ordered and bought separately in different sizes. This means the bridesmaid who is a size 12 on top and an 8 on the bottom won't have to settle for a dress that needs heavy-duty alterations. It usually results in dresses that fit and flatter much better, as well.

Essential

If a male friend is a member of the bride's entourage, he generally wears attire that is the same or very similar to the groomsmen. Depending on the bride's style, he may be differentiated with a special vest, bow tie, pocket square, or boutonnière (i.e., a different color or pattern or type than the other men).

Variations on a Theme

There is a recent trend referred to as "variations on a theme." This is when the bride chooses a specific dress color—usually from one dress designer—so the color remains consistent, and bridesmaids are given license to choose the dress style they feel most comfortable in. This works because designers typically offer a variety of dresses in the same choice of colors.

Sound like a great idea? Here's an example of how it works. The bride chooses a color and designer. The bridesmaids then get to select the dress style they prefer. The bridesmaid with perfectly chiseled arms may choose the spaghetti-strap number, while the bride with the impressive décolletage may choose the dress with the plunging neckline. This allows bridesmaids to choose a dress that's personally flattering and comfortable. These dresses may also come with additional options such as shawls or jackets for bridesmaids who wish to cover up a bit more. It all works because the dresses are the same color.

Who Chooses?

Let's cut to the chase. What is the process of choosing a dress, and how can you encourage your bride to choose attire with options? It's all up to the bride. Some brides will take along all their bridesmaids to choose a dress, though this method may be a bit daunting. The probability that five or more women would settle upon one dress and color in a single shopping trip seems near impossible.

Alert

Another important note if you choose this route is that the lengths of the dresses are the same, for example, all tea length or all floor length. Matching color and length allow for uniformity as well as a sense of individual style.

More likely, the bride will shop with her maid of honor or mother to narrow down the choices and colors; then, she may solicit the opinions of all her bridesmaids. Or she may simply decide upon one dress unilaterally, informing you later about her choice. The considerate bride will have kept everyone's interests in mind—including everyone's shape, size, and personal style—in order to choose a dress that all her bridesmaids will feel comfortable wearing.

The Lowdown on Styles

Bridesmaid dresses—as most dresses—will differ by length, silhouette, and fabric.

The following are some of the more popular choices in each of these categories.

LENGTH

- **Floor length:** This is the most popular length among bridesmaid dresses. As the name implies, this dress will fall approximately one inch from the floor.
- **Ankle length:** A bit shorter than floor length, this style just shows the ankles.
- **Tea length:** Shorter still than ankle length, tea length falls just at the mid-shin or a bit below.

SILHOUETTE

- **Ball gown:** Think Cinderella. Ball gowns are characterized by a tight, fitted bodice; a very full skirt; and a fitted, defined waistline.
- **A-line:** This is an extremely popular style among bridesmaid dresses, as it fits many body types comfortably. This dress has two vertical seams that start at the shoulders, flaring with an "A" shape to the floor. The dress typically skims the body without fitting snugly in any one location.
- **Empire:** Also called empire waist. This dress is defined by its very high waistline, which falls right under the bust. The skirt falls from there, and is usually straight and fairly slim.
- **Sheath:** Tight and fitted from top to bottom, this dress may flare near the ankles.

FABRICS

- **Linen:** A popular fabric for spring and summer bridesmaid dresses; lightweight fabric that wrinkles easily; best suited to a daytime event.

- **Satin:** This is a year-round bridesmaid dress fabric, also very popular. Smooth with a high sheen; cool to the touch.
- **Silk:** This strong fabric only looks delicate. It is smooth and sometimes has a sheen; traditionally quite expensive.
- **Chiffon:** Sheer, largely transparent material often used in layers; creates a very soft, feminine effect in dresses.
- **Taffeta:** A stiffer fabric with a small, crisscross rib; smooth and usually shiny like satin.
- **Brocade:** A heavier fabric; usually woven with an intricate design.

 **Question**

What should I do with the bridesmaid dress after I've worn it?
If you're lucky enough to like the dress, keep it and wear it again! You may consider taking it to a consignment shop to earn a little money back. Or check in your area for charities that accept donations of formal wear to pass on to high school girls that cannot afford dresses for their school dances.

On the rare occasion, a bride will allow her bridesmaids to choose their own destiny by shopping for their own dresses. She may give you one simple parameter, such as color or length, or she may let you have completely free reign. And while this is every bridesmaid's dream, it is also quite rare. If you are lucky enough to choose your own dress, you will obviously be able to pick something that's flattering and in your specific price range—always a welcome opportunity.

Finishing the Look

A bridesmaid is not made by dress alone! Once the dress is selected, there are a few more components that will make the entire ensemble complete. To create and complete the image of the picture-perfect bridesmaid, you are going to need to accessorize and beautify!

Accessorize Me!

The first part of finishing the look is the accessories. So, just what will you need to be fully accessorized? Typically, a bridesmaid wears a set of matching jewelry, shoes, and carries a coordinating handbag. Additionally, there may be hair accessories, such as a beautiful fabric flower or crystal-encrusted hair pin.

 Fact

If you are lucky, and as it often happens, the brides will purchase some of the accessories for you as your bridal party gift. This is a common and very bridesmaid budget-friendly idea!

Beautiful Bridesmaids

With a dress and a full accessory wardrobe in hand, it is time to complete the look. Professional hair and makeup styling adds the perfect touch to any ensemble. However, this does come with a price. If it is in the bride's budget and it is important enough to her to have a uniform group of ladies, she may budget for this, leaving you responsible for simply showing up on the wedding day. On the other hand, she may offer this as an additional service, for an additional cost.

Professional services like this are wonderful, but if it is not provided and just not in your own budget, be sure you are able to apply appropriate makeup and fashion a formal enough hair-style for the big day. You may want to make a trip to the makeup counter at the local department store and consult your own hair stylist for some tips.

✸ Essential

If you will be getting your hair and makeup profession-ally styled, be sure to bring a button-front shirt to wear while you are having your hair and makeup done. It is easily removed, so you can get into your dress without messing up your hair or smudging your lipstick.

Don't Forget a Thing!

As a bridesmaid, you have a lot of responsibility. It would be awful to forget an important detail of the bridesmaid's ensemble on the wedding day. With the help of this handy checklist, you will be well on your way to being a prepared bridesmaid!

BRIDESMAIDS' CHECKLIST

❑ Dress
❑ Hair accessories
❑ Handbag
❑ Hoisery (two pairs)
❑ Jewelry
❑ Makeup and hair-styling products
❑ Perfume
❑ Proper undergarments
❑ Shoes
❑ Toiletries (including deodorant)

CHAPTER 4

Always a Bridesmaid . . .

There are countless special circumstances that may come to light when serving as a bridesmaid. Usually, your good judgment will guide you, but from time to time you may feel a bit stymied, unsure of how to proceed. As you are dealing with a friend or family member, you need to maintain the highest possible level of diplomacy along the way, without compromising yourself in the process. All you need is some guidance and a little advice on how to deal with some common scenarios you may encounter.

The Pregnant Bridesmaid

You're pregnant . . . and the bride knew it when she asked you to be a bridesmaid, or you became pregnant partway through your bridesmaid stint and you need to break the news to the bride. Either way, some issues will arise. So how, if at all, will your pregnancy affect the wedding and your role as bridesmaid?

 **Essential**

> So you're pregnant. You're still working, still exercising—there's no reason you can't still be a bridesmaid. Embrace and enjoy it; at least you'll stand out from the other bridesmaids. Just be sure to tell the bride before she hears it elsewhere.

As with everything else in your life, being pregnant shouldn't make that much of an impact. That said, many brides—try as they might to avoid it—still have that "It's all about me" mentality, and a pregnant bridesmaid is not what they envisioned. "What if she 'ruins' the photos?" "What if the dress she has to wear looks matronly?" "What if she stands out too much?" Every once in a while, you see signs of how that engagement ring affects their better judgment.

If you suspect you're dealing with a bride who has this viewpoint (and you become pregnant) and she decides she'd rather you didn't participate any longer (and you suspect her reasons are entirely shallow), accept her wishes gracefully. Then run like mad. This woman is not your friend, and you're better off realizing this now than later. A bride who cares more for the aesthetics of her wedding day than she does about being surrounded by close friends and family is truly selfish.

On the other hand, there may be some circumstances when the bride may be acting altruistically. Maybe you've had a difficult pregnancy, have been ill, or are stressed out. There is a chance she's trying to let you off easy, so she doesn't add more stress to your load. If you suspect this is her motive, or you're not entirely sure, have an open talk with her. As with any conflict or misunderstanding, it's the only way you'll get honest answers.

Bad Timing

The only pregnancy issue that might legitimately affect your serving out your duties is timing. Obviously, if your due date falls on the same day as the wedding, you may have a problem. If the wedding is out of town, for instance, your doctor may advise against traveling for two weeks to a month before your due date (if travel involves flying). That will prevent you from walking down that aisle, whether you want to or not. So what should you do?

 Fact

If you know that you're pregnant when you're asked to be a bridesmaid, let the bride know as soon as possible. If you haven't told anyone yet, then tell her as soon as you officially announce it. Unless it's a travel issue or a conflicting due date, it shouldn't make a difference.

If it is an issue of bad timing but the wedding is in or around your hometown, the issue is a bit trickier. Suppose your due date is very close to the wedding date. You'll be on the brink of giving birth when the wedding takes place. There's a good chance you won't be feeling up to the stress of a wedding this close to your due date, and it would be a shame if you invested in a dress, shoes, and accessories only to give birth two days before the wedding and miss the whole thing.

If the wedding is a few hours away, you may also be hesitant to stray too far from your doctor or hospital. Special circumstances like these require careful deliberation. Talk to the bride and make her aware of the situation. If you simply know you won't feel up to it, most brides will find a very late-term pregnancy a perfectly legitimate excuse to decline.

The Dress

Luckily, you're not the first pregnant woman to serve as a bridesmaid—nor will you be the last. Most bridal salons and bridesmaid dress shops offer expert advice on the best styles for a pregnant bridesmaid, as well as expertise on predicting what your correct size will be at the time of the wedding. Obviously, you may not be able to dictate the dress style—the bride may have already done that—but if you have some say or if the bride is allowing you to choose your own style, an empire-waist dress is probably your best bet. This style dress, which has a skirt that falls from immediately below the bust line, will allow plenty of room for a growing belly to fit comfortably.

🅔✔ Fact

While many ladies may still be able to fit into a regular (nonmaternity) dress, there is one aspect you must consider. As your belly grows, it takes up some of that front fabric, causing the front hem of your dress to rise. Be sure the seamstress takes this into account.

Other styles, such as an A-line, will also work. For any style that isn't a maternity cut, you'll need to order a much larger size to accommodate your belly, and then have the bust and shoulders of the dress taken in by a seamstress or tailor.

🔔 Alert

If you're pregnant, be sure to solicit advice from the consultants at the dress shop before ordering your dress. They have the experience to predict what size you'll need five months from now.

You may also suggest to the bride that you have your dress custom made, using the same fabric and color chosen for the rest of the bridesmaid dresses. This way you can more easily gauge the correct size (you won't have to guesstimate what you'll look like six months in advance if you have the dress made a few weeks before the wedding) and you'll have a dress specifically designed for maternity wear. That means there's space for the belly but the rest of the dress will fit normally, unlike a nonmaternity bridesmaid dress, which will be too big in the bust, shoulders, and hips because you've ordered a significantly larger size.

The Newly Engaged Bridesmaid

So you're a bridesmaid . . . and also a bride-to-be! Congratulations. This is one wedding season you won't soon forget. Certainly, the fact that you've become engaged shouldn't affect serving out your role as bridesmaid. However, life can become stressful and overwhelming when trying to plan your own wedding's events, not to mention juggling shower plans, bachelorette party plans, and dress fittings for the other bride in your life, too. If this describes your situation, stop and take a deep breath, and get organized.

As with any other life situation, wise use of your time will be your greatest asset when balancing all your responsibilities. Be careful to avoid the most obvious pitfall—neglecting your bridesmaid duties now that you're a bride-to-be. It's easily done in the face of all the other details you need to arrange, but you don't want to let the bride down, or the other bridesmaids. After all, now that you're a bride yourself you can appreciate the value of everyone's enthusiastic participation, right?

Essential

If you're serving as bridesmaid and planning your own wedding at the same time, be sure not to neglect your bridesmaid duties. Just as you're counting on your own bridesmaids, the other bride is counting on you.

Noncompete Clause

When planning your own wedding, you should also avoid eclipsing your friend's/sister's/cousin's plans with your own. That means you should avoid setting your own wedding date to fall, say, a week before her wedding. Refrain from choosing a similar dress or one the exact same color, and don't plan your wedding for the same wedding location or one that competes. These actions would inevitably be viewed with great annoyance. In addition, consider the dates of the other bride's shower(s), bachelorette party, and other preparties when finalizing the dates for your own soirees.

So Many Brides, So Little Time

You've gone to school, then off to college. You got a "real" job, and then another. You've joined clubs and networked. Then poof! Suddenly, it seems someone from each social circle is engaged. Not only that, but all of their wedding dates fall within weeks of each other. Between your friends, your family, and your boyfriend's friends and family, you've even been invited to multiple weddings on the same day! What's a good friend to do?

This is a dilemma you will inevitably encounter at some point in your life. For some reason, it just seems to happen this way—you might even call it wedding season! Or you could blame it on pheromones, or even categorize it as aggressive husband hunting, but with friends of approximately the same age, this phenomenon will happen, and it may end up adversely affecting you. After all, you can't be two places at once.

Dueling Dates

So how do you prioritize which weddings you'll attend? If you've been asked to be a bridesmaid in any of these weddings, they should take immediate priority over the weddings where you'll be a regular guest. In other words, if you're invited to two weddings in the same weekend and you've been asked to be a bridesmaid in one of them, it's clear which one you'll need to attend. Sure, you'll be bummed to miss the other wedding, but you're an honored guest at this one, and that comes first.

Now, here is the tough part. What if you're asked to be a bridesmaid in two weddings on the same day? Does this seem impossible? Unfortunately, it has been known to happen. If this happens, you'll have to do some serious soul searching. Choosing between friends is never easy, and it will be difficult to break the news to the bride whose wedding you won't be attending. To make up for your absence at the wedding, make a valiant effort to travel to town before the wedding, attending the bridal shower and bachelorette party. Your honesty and efforts should pay off, and you can remain close with no hard feelings.

❓ Question

What's proper etiquette if I'm invited to two weddings in one day?
Some say you should attend the wedding whose invitation you received first. Others say to choose the event of the person you're closer with. If you can, make an appearance at both; if not, use your good judgment to make your decision.

If you face a situation like this, honesty is the best policy. Even if you can't be at one of the weddings, you can fulfill your prewedding bridesmaid responsibilities, like helping to throw a shower or assisting in the wedding plans. In the end, being a good friend will always override bad circumstances or unfortunate coincidences.

Oh So Popular!

Of course, being asked to be a bridesmaid in more than one wedding can cause some fallout, even if the weddings don't fall on the same day. As you've learned, being in one wedding is an expense—two or three in a single season might be more than you can (financially) bear. If you have enough notice, your first strategy is to begin saving early. Put away a specific amount of money each month to ensure you'll have the proper funds when the day comes. That means figuring in the cost of the dress, showers, bachelorette parties, and travel expenses.

Putting some of these expenses onto a credit card is also an option, though not highly recommended, as you'll end up paying a ridiculous amount of interest for the privilege of using the money now. A better bet might be a no- or low-interest loan from your parents, if they're willing and able to provide it.

If you truly know you cannot afford to be in all of these bridal parties, simply let the brides know. Again, you may need to choose between brides, and this may be an extremely difficult decision. Let your heart and conscience guide you. If it's very important to the bride, perhaps she'll offer to subsidize some of your expenses or to give you an alternative honored role, such as doing a wedding-day reading. That way you can still be part of the festivities without the financial obligation.

 Fact

It's not uncommon to serve as bridesmaid multiple times within a short time span. And while it may get a bit expensive, remember that it's an honor that you've been included in your friends' or family members' once-in-a-lifetime event.

Confronting Your Inner Bride

The most challenging circumstance you may face as a bridesmaid is actually your complete lack of circumstances; namely, you're quite single and not all that happy about it. While you may be thrilled for your friend, you cannot help feeling a little "off," especially if being married and beginning this chapter of your life is important to you. If this is the case, you are going to need to have a talk with that bride inside of you—she may need to be put in her place, for a while anyway.

Single Studies

Maybe you've just ended a long-term relationship. Maybe you're in the middle of a dry spell. Whatever the situation, you feel as if it's a couple's world and you're not part of it. Now you have been asked to be a part of someone else's celebration of love. Well, it may stink, but you have two choices: deal with the situation as a responsible, mature adult, or gracefully decline immediately. Even if all you really want is your own celebration, do not rain on your friend's parade!

🅔❗ Alert

Difficult as it may be, try not to let wedding fever over-come you. It's natural to imagine yourself in the bride's position, but don't let it affect your self-esteem or your own romantic relationship.

So how do you handle a situation when you feel as if the old cliché was written just for you: "Always a bridesmaid, never a bride"? First of all, let's put things into perspective. Life is never perfect for everyone at any one time. Everyone, even the bride, has had her "moments," too. It is simply her time right now. At the risk of sounding like your mother or grandmother, your day will come.

Your Status (Does Not) Count

Maybe your "always a bridesmaid" status has a slightly different twist, however. Maybe you're not single at all. Maybe you've been dating the same guy for quite a long time, and you've watched as girlfriend after girlfriend has gotten engaged before you. When will your time come? Should you dump your boyfriend after all the time you've invested? Should you give him an ultimatum?

✴ Essential

> If you are feeling anxious or overwhelmed, give yourself some time to determine what's causing your anxiety. Is it the wedding hoopla that's making you crazy, or are your anxieties based in reality? Is marriage something you really want with this person, or do you just long to plan a wedding and reap all the attention that comes with it? Be honest and the answer will be clear.

Unfortunately, your friend's circumstances can force long-latent issues like this one to the surface. Because when your sister and your best friend are planning their weddings, it's difficult not to imagine yourself in a similar situation, and to start questioning the circumstances in your own life. Don't dump your boyfriend. And DON'T give him an ultimatum. Sometimes, in the frenzy of planning a friend's wedding, your feelings can become confused. Then again, sometimes they're a totally legitimate wake-up call.

Attitude Matters

Regardless of your conclusions, you cannot make this wedding about you. Show enthusiasm and commitment as a bridesmaid for your friend or family member's wedding, and put your all into making this the best wedding experience it can be. The consideration you show will come back in spades when it's finally your time to wed. A bad attitude—or a perceived bad attitude—can be a friendship-breaker. A competitive relationship, silent resentment, and hurt feelings will do no one any good at all.

The point to all of this? Feelings of envy are a normal part of life, but letting these feelings control and ruin a perfectly good friendship is unnecessary and immature. You should never allow someone's good fortune to throw a dark shadow on a friendship. However, if you sense your feelings of envy are getting out of control—causing you outright depression or anger—it may be time to get some additional help. Try talking to a trusted friend, clergy member, or a therapist for objective advice. There's no sense in suffering when help is readily available.

Taming Bridezilla

Society has long accepted the notion of the blushing bride playing princess for a day, and the wedding industry has perpetuated this fantasy, promoting a no-holds-barred expectation when it comes to spending time, money, and resources in pursuit of this "dream." The most well-meaning brides often turn beast-like when it comes to planning their weddings. What exactly are the roots of this phenomenon? And how can you make it disappear . . . quickly?

Essential

Don't accept Bridezilla's abuse just because you're her bridesmaid. If her behavior violates the normal code of friendship, it's unacceptable during her engagement as well. Remember—you're her bridesmaid, not her punching bag!

Who Is She?

Bridezilla may go into deep debt to throw her wedding. She may throw multiple tantrums to get her way with her parents or fiancé. She's the bride who has put years of thought into her wedding day, but barely minutes into the days and years that will follow it. She's the bride who's alienating her parents, in-laws, fiancé, and other interested parties because there's only one way to throw this wedding—her way. She's probably the bride fighting with her mother, her future mother-in-law, or her fiancé as you read this sentence.

 Fact

Perhaps your Bridezilla is normally a sane, rational girl. As her good friend, it may be necessary to call her out on her dreadful behavior, especially if it's beginning to affect her relationships with others. Guess what? She may not even realize it.

This pressure to achieve perceived perfection has had dire results on some brides in recent years, who will often go to extreme measures to ensure it happens. Brides may spend money they don't have, demand things no rational woman would demand, and think about the wedding day more than their impending marriage. And there you have it: the seemingly normal woman who goes ballistic during her engagement.

Is This Normal?

Now, it's important to draw a distinction between the normal, enthusiastic bride and Bridezilla. You'll find Bridezilla, however, in a stratosphere beyond the normal bride. That's because Bridezilla often creates stress for herself and for those around her with demands and expectations that go beyond the norm. Planning any kind of wedding comes with a certain amount of stress and pressure. It also breeds excitement about seemingly minute details like napkin colors and favors. Add this planning stress and excitement to work and family responsibilities, and it's normal for any bride to experience highs and lows, including moments when she's frustrated, stressed out, depressed, or simply numb.

🅴 Alert

As a bridesmaid, it's your duty to help the bride with wedding-related tasks; it's when she crosses the line and you begin suffering for the sake of her wedding that her behavior becomes unacceptable.

Too often, Bridezilla treats her friends more like hired assistants than as trusted confidantes. She demands that all her bridesmaids buy very expensive dresses, jewelry, and shoes. She has you running wedding-related errands for her three to four times per week. She drops last-minute snafus on your plans, and may even ask you to shed a pound or two. Bridezilla knows no bounds.

Out of Control

The bottom line is that being a bridesmaid shouldn't become a daily obligation. It shouldn't give the bride license to act in ways that would normally be judged as rude or inconsiderate just because her actions are wedding related.

Ultimately, the bride should never make requests that cause her bridesmaids to feel uncomfortable or pressured to do something they wouldn't normally do, like asking her bridesmaids to get identical, chin-length bobs a few weeks before the wedding or dye their hair blonde so they all match. Don't laugh, it has happened!

What Should You Do?

Remember, being a bridesmaid is always voluntary. Hard as it may be, there may be circumstances that justify dropping out of the bridal party. Before you do, though, be sure to communicate your feelings to the bride. There's a chance she may not even realize she's been behaving badly, and if she's reasonable she'll try to correct her actions rather than lose a bridesmaid—or a friend.

Essential

If you have a relationship with the bride's mother (or father), you may even be able to go to them for help in taming Bridezilla. Sometimes, these observations will be taken better from a parent. You will, however, need to consider the relationships of all involved before going this route.

If you suspect the bride will never see the error of her ways, try this approach. Tell her that under the present circumstances you're unable to serve as a supportive, enthusiastic bridesmaid, so you'd rather not be a hypocrite and continue on. Without accusing her outright, this will get your point across that she's acting like a complete ninny, and perhaps it will prompt her to engage in a little self-reflection.

Girl Trouble

Bridezilla? No way. You've got the bride from heaven . . . it's the bridesmaids from hell who are causing you angst. Who are these chicks, anyway? Get almost any group of people together to complete a task and there's bound to be some conflict. Like every office breeds politics and every sorority breeds enmity, every bridal party has its touchy moments. Tina's not pitching in enough; Jackie's trying to control everyone; Maura's lazy; Angela won't stop complaining.

e! Alert

Be careful of your tone in e-mails, especially if the group of bridemaids has not met in person. Sarcasm and some humor doesn't always "read" correctly in e-mail, and you may end up with some hurt feelings.

What's the Problem?

If you're planning a shower and/or bachelorette party, any number of scenarios may arise among your group. The following outlines some of the more common ones, with quick solutions that can smooth things over for the whole bridal party, including the bride, who should never be burdened with the prospect of feuding bridesmaids.

The Indifferent Bridesmaid

This girl doesn't take the initiative on anything. While the rest of the bridesmaids snap up tasks like making shower decorations, taking on cooking duties, or organizing games, this bridesmaid hasn't volunteered once to help out.

Solution: Delegate tasks to her. She may not even realize she's slacking; some people simply need to be told what to do. Rather than resenting her, simply get her involved, and then get over it.

The Take-Control Bridesmaid

The maid of honor's supposed to be running the show, but this bridesmaid is making independent moves with shower and bachelorette party plans, and demanding the rest of the girls' help. Who should you be listening to?

Fact

Bridesmaids should work as a team to complete tasks such as shower and bachelorette party planning. No one bridesmaid (with the exception of the maid of honor) should have to handle the brunt of the responsibility.

Solution: Hold a bridesmaid pow-wow. The maid of honor should ultimately be calling the shots, but perhaps she's delegated some tasks to this bridesmaid and you were simply unaware. Or maybe your initial impression is correct, and this busybody is just a rogue bridesmaid acting inappropriately. There's only one way to find out. Meet, and bring up plans among the group. When they're brought to the light of day with everyone in attendance, plans will inevitably get ironed out, and everyone will have a say.

The Troubled Bridesmaid

Perhaps she's gotten into some financial trouble or she's having some problems with drinking and/or drugs. Or maybe she's simply going through a bout of depression. No matter what the problem, being a bridesmaid has not been high on her list of priorities.

Solution: Be a friend. Try to help her with the root cause of her problem, if possible, or steer her toward someone who can help. And try not to attack her for shirking her bridesmaid duties, even if it means taking up some of the slack yourself. Being put on the defensive by you or the other bridesmaids may only add to her current burden.

The Absent Bridesmaid

This bridesmaid is a regular no-show for parties, showers, and other wedding-related events. You know that her behavior has been hurtful and disappointing to the bride. Is there anything you should do?

Solution: Use your judgment. If you think a few well-chosen, nonconfrontational words will affect this bridesmaid's behavior, then offer them. If you know that talking to her will do no good, though, don't get involved. It may only cause more problems and tension for the bride in the long run.

The Bitchy Bridesmaid

You've just met her, and already you can't stand her. Or you've known her forever and you can stand her even less. She's selfish and snobbish, and frankly, you can't even believe the bride's still friends with her.

Solution: There is none. Unfortunately, there are plenty of unpleasant people we have to deal with in life, and it's not up to you to change this woman's personality. Try to put up with her no matter how you feel about her, for the sake of the bride. After all, the bride shouldn't have to deal with bridesmaid conflict, along with everything else she's juggling right now. If possible, give this bridesmaid the benefit of the doubt. Maybe it's simply a long history of disdain and indifference toward each other that's affecting your attitudes. After all, you do have the bride in common. Give her one more chance, and see whether she'll warm up—maybe she's simply been on the defensive all this time.

The Broke Bridesmaid

She's constantly complaining about money, and the complaining continues no matter how budget conscious you all are. While planning the shower and bachelorette party, she's still singing the blues about her contribution.

Solution: Perhaps she really is in bad financial straits, or maybe she's just cheap. If you know her at all, you've probably got a good gauge on the situation. If she really is having some problems, try to give her a break. Get together with the rest of the bridesmaids and see if you can cover her share, or plan a less extravagant event. If you suspect she's just being tight with her money, compromise on the cost of the affair—then be firm about her contribution. You're all in this together.

Question

I have tried and tried to settle the squabbles between the bridesmaids to no avail. Should I ask the bride to step in?

Calling on the bride is a last resort. If these ladies really won't settle in for the ride, it is unfortunate. If after a nice long heart-to-heart there is still a problem, ask the groom if he may be able to plead the case, or maybe the bride's mother may be able to help as well. Ask them to keep this confidential.

She Just Isn't Cooperating

How do you promote diplomacy among a group of women who may or may not know each other? The answer is patience. Although it's the maid of honor who finds herself in the hot seat when it comes to directing and organizing the group, as a bridesmaid, you can also be an ambassador of goodwill among the girls. Miss Nuptial Congeniality, so to speak.

In a situation like this, it is really important for the maid of honor to take charge. Now more than ever, a strong leader is important. The last thing you want to do is drag the bride into this minor fiasco. If the maid of honor cannot cut it, talk to her and make a plan—you may have to be the new de facto leader. Ultimately, the most important thing is that the bride is not dragged into this situation.

CHAPTER 5

Fun, Fabulous Showers

One bridesmaid duty most ladies already know about is helping to plan a shower for the bride. If for some reason you didn't know that . . . you do now! Like everything else, a bridal shower should reflect the style and scale of the wedding. No longer always the traditional, somewhat formal, women-only gatherings they once were, showers today may include guests numbering from 10 to 100, they may be held on a weekend or a week-night, and they may even include—gasp!—men as guests.

Bridal Showers 101

It seems easy on the surface—pick a locale, send out some invites, buy some food, buy a present—the shower is done, right? Wrong! There are definitely a few more complexities that need to be explored before you get moving on planning this bridal shower.

History of the Shower

It has been said that the first shower was held in Holland hundreds of years ago. A Dutch woman fell in love with a poor miller who had become impoverished by generously giving away his goods and money to those in need. Her father did not approve of this marriage, which he felt was beneath her, preferring she marry a wealthier man whom his daughter did not love.

 Fact

Legend has it an Englishwoman brought the concept of a shower into the modern age. Wishing she could give a friend a more substantial engagement gift, but without the means to do so, she threw a party at which everyone could shower the bride with gifts all at once.

He tried to get his way by refusing to give a dowry to the poor miller, knowing the two would not have the means to establish a home. When the townspeople heard of the couple's fate, they decided to take matters into their own hands, "showering" the couple with the household items they needed to make a start, thus repaying the miller's longtime generosity.

What's the Point?

The main objective of the shower is to help furnish the bride (and groom) with the household items she'll need to start making a home. The typical bridal shower is held either at a small function hall or in someone's home, depending on the size of the guest list. Most bridal showers involve food and games. Traditionally, the guests were women only, but today fiancés are welcome. Coed showers continue to be popular; just try to avoid gender-specific activities and bridal shower games. Stick to a gender-neutral theme, as well. For example, lingerie showers are bad ideas for coed shindigs.

Essential

While it is considered poor etiquette to include any gift-registry information with a wedding invitation, the opposite is true for a bridal shower; after all, that is the intended point of it. Feel free to tactfully include this information with the shower invitation.

Today's showers are more open to interpretation. Bridesmaids and family members are hosting unique gatherings that incorporate creative activities, unique foods and cocktails, and fun new games. For the bridesmaid, today's looser interpretation of showers can both complicate and ease your planning duties. The one thing all showers should have in common, however, is that they serve a practical purpose—gifts for the bride—as well as providing a forum to celebrate the upcoming nuptials.

Plan It!

Yes, all of this wonderful planning comes with a price—time and money. If you need help planning this event, or financing it, talk to the bridesmaids well in advance of the proposed shower date. A bridal shower should be held one to two months before the wedding date. Avoid scheduling it too close to the wedding, as this is an extremely busy time. Be sure to consult with the bride (and her mother) before making the date official.

 Fact

Showers are most commonly held on a Saturday or Sunday, usually in the late morning or early afternoon, but a growing trend is to host a shower on a weeknight or weekend evening. Evening showers are often a bit looser and more casual than the typical Sunday afternoon brunch.

Planning Checklist

Before you even begin determining the style or planning the specific shower details, it will help to know exactly what elements you'll need to think about when planning any type of shower. The following checklist is meant to help you organize your thoughts, as well as the details, as you begin the planning process.

VENUE
- ❏ Home
- ❏ Restaurant
- ❏ Country club
- ❏ Banquet facility

❑ Outdoors
❑ Other: _____

GUEST LIST
❑ Family members
❑ Friends
❑ Bridal party
❑ Men
❑ Children

FOOD
❑ Lunch
❑ Brunch
❑ Dinner
❑ Hors d'oeuvres only
❑ Cake and sweets only
❑ Cake or specialty dessert (to accompany a meal)

DRINKS
❑ Nonalcoholic only
❑ Punch
❑ Wine
❑ Martinis
❑ Cocktails
❑ Beer

DECORATIONS
❑ Flowers
❑ Balloons
❑ Linens
❑ China
❑ Silver

❏ Glassware: _____
❏ Other: _____
❏ Entertainment: _____
❏ Favors/Prizes: _____
❏ Games: _____
❏ Activities: _____

Pay for It!

Oh yeah, showers don't come for free. Typically, the bridesmaids come together to plan and pay for a bridal shower. If you pool your resources, it shouldn't be too expensive to host a tasteful, fun shower that everyone will enjoy and that the bride will truly appreciate.

 Alert

Obviously, it would be rude to plan an expensive over-the-top shower without consulting anyone and then ask the bridesmaids to up the ante. You should definitely get their input before planning and demanding anything of them.

Narrow down your options, pinpoint some bridal preferences, choose the best style and size shower to suit your bride, and most importantly, determine your budget. Once these aspects are in place, ideas for specific themes, along with ideas for shower games, activities, and creative gifts will develop from there. So read ahead, get organized, and get ready to have some fun.

Expenses

How do you determine a budget when you don't even know what is included in a bridal shower? The following list is a compilation of the most common bridal shower expenses.

BRIDAL SHOWER EXPENSES
- Beverages
- Cake or specialty dessert
- Decorations
- Decorations (nonfloral)
- Entertainment
- Favors
- Flowers
- Food
- Games (supplies for)
- Games (prizes for)
- Gift
- Linens
- Location
- Paper goods/products
- Place settings

Alert

Just like a wedding, factors such as the number of guests and the time of day greatly affect the overall budget. The menu expected with a dinner event is much more expensive than that associated with a brunch or lunch menu.

Laying the Groundwork

Now that you have been introduced to the basics in bridal showers, maybe you need a little guidance, a little nudge to put you on the road to planning bliss. The following questions will help you begin narrowing your focus regarding what type of shower you'd like to host, then narrow down some of the many options.

- What's your budget? Will you need help from the other bridesmaids, or do you want to foot the bill and throw the party yourself?
- Is the bride very traditional, or would she appreciate a creative twist?
- Will it be formal or casual?
- Do you feel it's important to serve a full meal?
- Can you cook, or will you get the help of a friend, family member, or caterer?
- Do you have enough space to host it at your own home, or is there another bridesmaid who does? (You can also ask a family member or friend if you can "borrow" their home for the day.)
- Would you prefer professionals handle everything, from beginning to end?
- Will you host a theme shower?
- Are there unusual circumstances (the bride is pregnant, it's her second wedding, etc.)?
- Would you rather host a coed Jack-and-Jill shower? (These have grown increasingly popular in recent years.)
- Would an evening gathering be better than a daytime one?
- Are there lots of out-of-town guests to invite and accommodate? (Weekends might be best in this case.)

- Do you want to include party games?
- Do you want to incorporate any new traditions?

Defining Your Options

In recent years, more hosts have been throwing showers with creative themes, such as a wine-tasting or spa-themed shower. As you plan, feel free to be creative—your shower guests certainly won't mind attending a party that's a little different, and in fact it may be expected, with the bride's permission of course. (For more on themes, see the suggestions later in this chapter.)

Try Something New on for Size

It is a new world of weddings out there, and a new breed of bride and bridesmaids, so all bets are off. Ordinary and expected are out. Stylized and fun are in . . . with homage paid to tradition! No matter what the genesis, over the past fifty-plus years, showers have followed certain traditions and patterns that haven't varied a whole lot. These showers traditionally included these characteristics:

- Women only
- Held on a weekend morning or afternoon
- A light lunch and dessert
- Ice-breaker games and/or activities
- Small gifts or favors for the guests
- Focused upon the bride opening her gifts

Styled for Her

The traditional shower, while enjoyable, doesn't suit every bride. For instance, some brides may not want to receive gifts at all. Some may prefer a male/female guest list, and some may hate the idea of playing games. And while it's easy to go with the traditional shower format outlined here, you may also wish to determine if your bride would take exception to some of these traditions—or if she would simply enjoy, or be more comfortable with, some new traditions.

✳ Essential

Follow the bride's personality as a guide to the type of shower you'll host. Feel free to break certain traditions if they don't fit with her tastes or expectations. For example, she may prefer a coed or no-gifts shower, both of which veer from tradition.

The number one most important thing is that you make this shower about and for the bride and her marriage. You may wish to talk to the bride directly to learn her preferences. Although she is supposed to be mainly hands off in the planning of her bridal shower, she may have her heart set on some specific shower ideas, and you should listen!

If the shower happens to be a surprise, you can use the following questions and answers to get some insight into what would make her happiest. The following questions will get you thinking about the bride's personality and interests.

- Does the bride's close social circle include male as well as female acquaintances?
- Does the bride prefer girls-only or mixed gatherings?
- Does attention and fuss make the bride uncomfortable?
- Is the bride typically more laid back and casual or more high maintenance?
- Is the bride very picky about what she eats and drinks?

- Does the bride like large, boisterous groups, or is she more comfortable among a small group of intimates?
- Are there a lot of bridesmaids, or just a few? (It's typically the case that the more bridesmaids, the larger the shower.)
- Which better represents the bride, Chardonnay and crudités, or beer and burgers?
- Is the bride a stickler for etiquette?

 Fact

If the shower is a surprise and you are still looking for some guidance, consult with the bride's mother or sister for some more details about what she expects. You can even ask the groom. What's important is to make her happy.

Setting the Tone

The answers to the above questions will obviously go a long way in determining what style shower she'd most enjoy. For instance, if she's a beer and burgers gal, she'll probably be more comfortable with a laid-back, casual shower than an English tea. And if she likes doing things by the book, she probably won't feel right about a shower with a wacky theme or unusual activities. So use your answers to these questions—and your instincts—to plan a shower the bride and everyone else will enjoy.

Ultimately, you should let the style of the bride's wedding and her own personal style guide you as you set the tone for the bridal shower. Yes, it is common sense, but all too often, when weddings come into play, common sense goes out the window.

Clearly, some of these options are limited by your budget and by your capabilities.

The Skinny on Themes

One of the decisions that will drive the remaining planning details is whether or not you are going to throw a theme shower. What is a theme shower, you ask? It's anything with an overriding concept or idea attached to it, beyond the expected shower activities. A theme shower needn't be complicated or involve special activities; you can fashion a theme around all the traditional shower activities, with a slight twist.

Question

As a bridesmaid, if I attend three showers, do I have to give three gifts?
Etiquette advises that no, you do not. But you may wish to consider giving one substantial gift, followed by two smaller gifts, so you won't feel as though you're arriving empty handed at any of the events.

One example of this scenario is a shower whose theme is gift-related only, like a round-the-clock shower. For this type of shower, each guest is assigned a different time of day; the gift they bring should correspond to that time of day. For example, a time of 11 P.M. might inspire a gift of lingerie or a popcorn popper. A time of 7 A.M. might inspire a coffee maker, a hair dryer, or an electric toothbrush.

You can limit this type of theme to gifts or expand it with decorations, favors, and food, too, if the spirit moves you. For example, you might give each guest a small clock or a calendar as favors; you might serve a cake that's been decorated to resemble a clock; or you might give the bride a countdown clock that counts the hours and minutes until her wedding day.

Pick a Theme, Any Theme

There are countless themes, ranging from fun and festive to downright seductive. Read ahead to find one that's perfect to incorporate into your celebration.

ABC Shower

At this shower, each guest is assigned a letter of the alphabet, and her gift should reflect that letter. For example, if she's assigned the letter "C," she might give the bride a clock or a Cuisinart or a Calphalon pan. The fun behind the alphabet shower lies in the creative lengths that guests will go to in fulfilling their assigned letter. Again, you can tie the theme into any other aspect of the shower, such as games, food, or decorations. Serve alphabet soup; give guests favors like magnetic poetry sets or bookmarks.

Fitness Shower

So the bride's an outdoorswoman or a sports buff. You know that she'd appreciate a new set of ski bindings ten times more than a new blender. There's just one thing to do—hold a fitness shower! For this theme, be sure to give guests some guidance on appropriate gifts. While most women have some insight in choosing glassware, many women won't have the first clue about choosing the right thermal wear. If possible, have the bride register for sports-related gifts at an all-purpose sports store like Sports Authority. If no store near you offers a formal registry service, see if they'll design a makeshift one for the special occasion. A privately owned local sports store might be more inclined to help out this way.

If you know that many of the guests are also sports-minded, incorporate some fitness-related activities into the shower. Take a hike, a bike ride, or play tennis with the group. Give nonsporting guests an alternative, such as arriving for food, drinks, and gift-giving afterward, or include them as drivers or spectators so no one feels left out.

Hobby Shower

The hobby shower is meant to encourage gift-giving related to the bride's favorite activities. This theme is perfect for the bride with lots of interests. It's also ideal for the bride and groom who've been on their own for a while and don't need to be set up with home essentials like towels, sheets, and cookware.

For example, maybe she loves to read or she's totally into scrapbooking, and she can't get enough yoga. Appropriate gifts in this case might include a reading lamp, a beautiful bookmark, a yoga membership, a yoga mat, fitness clothing, or scrapbooking accessories. In case guests aren't specifically aware, let them know the bride's interests on the invitation. Of course, the theme can also be extended to the groom's hobbies, too.

Once again, any of the hobbies can be incorporated into the shower activities, as well. You might have a scrapbooking session, or you can pay a yoga instructor to make a house call to your shower. As with anything, give guests who choose not to or who are unable to engage in the activity an option to do something else.

Lingerie Shower

This is the perfect shower for the bride who has everything. Typically, lingerie or "personal" showers are relatively small and intimate. After all, the bride may not feel comfortable opening and admiring lacy thongs and peek-a-boo teddies in front of her fiancé's grandmother. So if you're going to throw a lingerie shower, keep it small and intimate. Invite guests the bride feels comfortable with, such as her close girlfriends only. In addition to the aforementioned, gifts might include nighties, underwear, potpourri, lotions, perfumes, silk sheets, sexy books, and so on.

🅮 Alert

A lingerie shower is a popular theme, but also a private theme of sorts. If this is the theme you select, be sure to book a private room or venue or even have the shower at your home so as to not make anyone—shower-related or not—uncomfortable.

A lingerie shower is a very girly shower. As such, you may wish to keep it in theme. Serve champagne, strawberries, and truffles. Give out small lotions or perfumes as shower gifts. Play games you wouldn't play in mixed company. For example (if you think the bride will feel comfortable with it), invite everyone to tell her most risqué memory of the bride. Or have everyone write down their wildest experience, put it in a bowl, and have the bride read them one by one—guessing the author of each story. Create a serene, Victoria's Secret-type atmosphere with light classical music, aromatherapy candles, and low light. Of course, don't throw a lingerie shower or include any activities if you suspect it will make the bride uncomfortable. This is not the time to attempt to expand her horizons, even if you think it would be fun.

Holiday Shower

If the bride and groom already have many of the traditional shower gifts like linens and cookware, this is a fun shower theme. In this shower invitation, you'll assign each guest a specific holiday. Holidays might include Christmas, Halloween, Fourth of July, Flag Day, Rosh Hashanah, Easter, Hanukkah—choose whatever holidays the bride and groom celebrate.

Guests are instructed to bring a gift that relates to those holidays. For instance, a guest assigned the Fourth of July may give the bride and groom a set of grill tools or outdoor plates and bowls; for Christmas, gifts might include tree ornaments, decorations, a tree skirt, or a nativity set. This type of shower is a great way to help the bride and groom begin building a collection of holiday décor.

Essential

Before reserving a room or sending out invitations, be sure to check the shower date with the bride and her family. With so much going on, you don't want to risk scheduling the shower for the same day as another event.

To tie the theme into the shower celebration, get creative. Have a Christmas in July shower at which you serve Christmas cookies, decorate with a small Christmas tree, and sing Christmas carols. Invite Santa to make an appearance (disguise the groom or the bride's father) to present gifts to the bride or to give small gift-wrapped favors to each guest.

Conversely, have a Fourth of July in December party. Rent out a large indoor site where you can play indoor volleyball or tennis or rent a hotel's indoor pool room or spa room for a few hours, where you can lounge, swim, and have a bite to eat. Serve barbecue and drink summer cocktails.

Wine Shower

A wine shower is another great idea for the bride and groom who are already established with the household items they need, or if the bride is being given multiple showers and you want to host an event that's a little different from the others. For a wine shower, you guessed it—guests give wine as gifts to the bride. If the bride and groom are wine enthusiasts, this is a wonderful way to jumpstart a wine collection for their new home, or to supplement one they already have. Guests might bring local wines, specialty wines, bottles they've been saving—anything goes. They may also choose to bring wine-related gifts such as wine corks, wine openers, wine chillers, or wine glasses.

Of course, a wine shower wouldn't be much fun without a wine tasting. When you plan this shower, you may decide to host your own tasting at home, or if you're in proximity to a winery, you may want to hold the shower there. Wineries often offer tasting events, so be sure to call and negotiate on behalf of your group ahead of time. They may also provide food. If not, bring items such as crackers, cheeses, and finger foods to enjoy along with the wine and see if the winery can accommodate the group afterward for a light lunch—bring it yourself or have it catered. Give each guest a pretty wine cork as a party favor.

Activity Shower

The activity shower is a great idea for the bride who is looking for something different. For such a party, ten or fewer guests is preferable. This shower revolves around an activity such as ceramics, jewelry making, or cooking lessons. The venue can be a specialty shop where you can go with a small group and actually make things on site, using their materials. For example, at a ceramics shop, you can hand-paint plates, bowls, mugs, and other specialty items. To incorporate this activity into a shower, choose one style of bowl or plate for all the guests to work on, choose a color scheme, and then have everyone paint and design the piece with her own creative flair.

At the end of the shower, the bride is given all the bowls or plates as a set for a shower gift—a very personal offering with great memories attached to it. (This would also be a fun warm-up to a bachelorette party.)

Couples Shower

The couples or coed shower has grown increasingly popular in recent years. Clearly, as gender roles blur, so does the delineation between men and women when it comes to celebrating their union. To some, the idea of holding events that separate males from females seems in direct conflict with the idea of marriage and the partnership between husband and wife. Whether you have strong beliefs about the issue or you just think it would be fun, a couples shower is an all-inclusive alternative to celebrate the bride and groom's impending nuptials.

For a couples shower, you'll obviously wish to cater to both the men and the women of the group. For that reason, these gatherings usually resemble engagement parties more than ladies' showers. They can still include many of the traditional shower activities, but the attendance of men certainly rules out, say, serving cucumber finger sandwiches and water with lemon as the featured menu items.

Plan this shindig as you would any other mixed gathering, with the addition of gift giving as a featured activity. Yes, the bride should still engage in the traditional gift-opening session, except this time she's joined by the groom. While enjoyable for the women, you may wish to incorporate an activity that will simultaneously amuse the men during the gift-opening session, like eating. And before or after the gifts, you may also wish to include shower games tailored to both sexes, like this version of the Newlywed Game.

Fact

A couples shower is more like an engagement party, except that the couple is expected to open their gifts while they're at the event, like a traditional shower. It's the perfect alternative for the bride who has good friends who are both male and female.

As a fun activity, have two or three couples volunteer in advance to take part in competing against the bride and groom. Direct an impartial bridesmaid to ask each half of the couple the same questions in private immediately before the competition, so there's no cheating. The object is for the woman's answers to match the man's. Tailor the questions for your group. If it's an uptight group, for instance, try not to ask too many questions with the word "whoopee" in them. Questions might include these: What's your least favorite chore? What's your spouse-to-be's biggest pet peeve? What quality do you like most about your spouse-to-be? What's your anniversary, including the date and year? Be creative with your questions.

Put the answers to the questions on big sheets of paper so they can be compared against each other, with the shower guests as the "studio audience." The couple with the most matching answers and the most points wins a prize, which can be a gag gift or something of actual value. You may also wish to set up the bride and groom to win beforehand, by giving them the answer to a difficult "bonus" question. You'll get a lot of laughs when they actually get it right. Ask something they couldn't possibly know about each other, like the name of their first-grade teacher or their exact SAT scores.

Recipe Shower

If the bride does not want to receive shower gifts but the bridesmaids still want to honor her with a get-together, a recipe shower is a great option. You can do this a couple of ways. For either alternative, specify "no gifts" on the invitations. Your first option is to ask each guest to send you or another bridesmaid her favorite recipe prior to the shower date (a couple weeks in advance is recommended). You then use the recipes to create a personalized cookbook that will serve as a gift for the bride at the shower. Choose the craftiest or most computer-savvy bridesmaid to format and/or design the cookbook.

❓ Question

Are the bridesmaids expected to attend every shower?
The wedding party, as well as the mothers, should be invited to every shower, but they are not obligated to bring a gift to more than one shower.

The second alternative is to send each guest a special card or page on which to write the recipe. Then bind all the pages together for a beautiful keepsake with a personal touch—each individual's handwriting. Create a cover and pretty binding for a gift the bride will cherish for years to come.

Who's Coming?

You don't have to invite all the women who'll be at the wedding to your shower. Usually, bridal showers are much more about intimate get-togethers than grandiose affairs. You, your wedding attendants, family members, and five to thirty of your closest friends should make the party a success story. Multiple showers to accommodate different groups of friends, coworkers, and large families are not uncommon.

The Guest List

Before you even begin to plan your party's particulars, you should determine the guest list. Many factors contribute to developing the guest list, but the bride and her family should ultimately finalize this list.

 Fact

Unless the shower is a surprise, it is the bride's responsibility to compile a guest list (including addresses) and provide the names and locations of the stores where she is registered.

The first rule of thumb when throwing any shower is to invite only people who will also be invited to the wedding. You should never invite guests who will not make the final wedding list. They will feel as if they were only invited to the shower for their ability to proffer a gift, which is really not far off the mark.

The next step to help narrow down your list is to determine if the bride will be having any other showers. For example, if her aunts are throwing her a big, catered affair for fifty, then you may wish to plan a much smaller gathering of close friends and immediate family only. In other words, if the aunts have all the extended female relatives on the bride's and groom's sides covered, then it's perfectly okay to host a smaller, more intimate shower. If yours will be the bride's only shower, however, you'll probably wish to open it up to friends and family members of the bride and groom, so everyone can meet, greet, and celebrate in advance of the wedding.

e✔ Fact

In order to give guests, especially those from out of town, plenty of time to make arrangements to come to the shower, you should send out invitations four to six weeks in advance.

Of course, you may also decide to have a coed or couples shower, which will immediately double the size of your party. A safe guest list includes the bride's and groom's immediate family only, along with perhaps a few close friends. Or keep it among your contemporaries only and just invite the bride and groom's immediate social circle, including the bridesmaids and groomsmen. You may also wish to include the bride's and groom's parents so they can meet or mingle with everyone before the festivities.

Bridal Shower Guest List		
RSVP	Name	Address
1. ☐		
2. ☐		
3. ☐		
4. ☐		
5. ☐		
6. ☐		
7. ☐		
8. ☐		
9. ☐		
10. ☐		
11. ☐		
12. ☐		
13. ☐		
14. ☐		
15. ☐		
16. ☐		
17. ☐		
18. ☐		
19. ☐		
20. ☐		
21. ☐		
22. ☐		
23. ☐		
24. ☐		
25. ☐		

Bridal Shower Guest List		
RSVP	Name	Address
26. ☐		
27. ☐		
28. ☐		
29. ☐		
30. ☐		
31. ☐		
32. ☐		
33. ☐		
34. ☐		
35. ☐		
36. ☐		
37. ☐		
38. ☐		
39. ☐		
40. ☐		
41. ☐		
42. ☐		
43. ☐		
44. ☐		
45. ☐		
46. ☐		
47. ☐		
48. ☐		
49. ☐		
50. ☐		

You're Invited!

So what should the shower invitation look like? Unlike the wedding invitation, shower invitations do not have to be extremely formal. You can find an array of predesigned styles at stationery stores, party supply stores, wedding-planning resource centers, and even online! Many of these options offer printing, but the good old-fashioned way of filling them in by hand is still acceptable.

Essential

To save time and energy, you may also decide to purchase preprinted invitations with all the vital information. These can be customized and ordered at a wedding stationery store.

An even less expensive option is to print the invitations yourself. With the evolution of personal color printers, the quality is appropriate for most invitations. Plus, you can purchase invitation "shells" with pretty designs at office supply stores and wedding stationery stores and lay out the text to fit the graphics for a professional look at a do-it-yourself price.

The following should be included on the shower invitation:

- Name of the bride
- Type of party (bridal shower, couples' shower, etc.)
- Date and time
- Address
- Name of hostess(es)
- RSVP date
- Phone number and e-mail address for RSVP

- Theme information, if applicable
- Shower registry information (optional)

Gifts Galore

There's no confusion about the objective of a shower—it's meant to set up the bride with the things she needs for her new home. Presumably, therefore, no one should really care if registry information is included; in fact, it might even make her life a bit easier. Etiquette states that this is acceptable, but there will definitely be detractors who think including this information is inappropriate. If you're uncertain, solicit the bride's opinion. If she's uncomfortable with including the information, then don't do it.

 Fact

Ask the bride for a list of locations where she is registered to include with her shower invitation. Be sure to have her register at appropriate stores if there is a theme, such as registering at a cooking specialty store if the theme is gourmet.

The most important thing to remember for any shower is to assign someone the task of keeping track of gifts. If you're in on the planning, bring this book with you and assign someone you trust with the task of filling out the following recorder (or do it yourself). This way, the bride will know who gave which gift when the time comes to send out the thank-you notes.

Gift Recorder		
Name	**Description of Gift**	**Thank-You Note Sent?**
1.		☐
2.		☐
3.		☐
4.		☐
5.		☐
6.		☐
7.		☐
8.		☐
9.		☐
10.		☐
11.		☐
12.		☐
13.		☐
14.		☐
15.		☐
16.		☐
17.		☐
18.		☐
19.		☐
20.		☐
21.		☐
22.		☐
23.		☐
24.		☐
25.		☐

CHAPTER 6

An Unforgettable Bachelorette Party

Bachelorette parties have a bad reputation, but there is no reason that you must follow in *that* tradition. Think beyond the legends of drinking and carousing, and be more creative and adventurous . . . unless, of course, the aforementioned is what you had in mind. The bachelorette party is all about showing the bride a good time. In recent years, bachelorette parties have evolved in different directions to more accurately reflect the bride's sensibilities.

The What and Why of a Bachelorette Party

While the bachelor party has been around for a long time, the bachelorette party only became popular in the latter half of the twentieth century, probably due to the sexual revolution, when women decided that going a little wild before the wedding was their "right," too. Traditionally, sometime before the wedding, friends of the bride and groom take them out (separately, of course) to celebrate the end of their single days. These parties are not mandatory, but your single friends might be disappointed if you don't want one.

ⓔ✹ Essential

These parties were once held the night before the wedding, but now they're usually held a week or two before the ceremony, thus ensuring that the members of the wedding party will be fully recovered from their hangovers in time for the wedding.

The maid of honor, together with the other bridesmaids, is in charge of the bachelorette party. The organizer may ask all attendees for contributions to pay for the shindig, and since party guests are not expected to bring gifts, it's perfectly all right to do so, as long as all the invitees are told about the plans and financial arrangements in advance.

The Makings of a Great Party

While some brides still like the idea of a wild and crazy night on the town, other brides see the bachelorette party as an opportunity to relax and spend quality time with her closest friends and family members before she ties the knot. No matter what, all bachelorette parties have one thing in common: they're events that bring the bride's girlfriends and/or close female relatives together for a day or evening (or weekend) of fun and companionship before the wedding.

Planning and hosting a bachelorette party has become another of the bridesmaids' responsibilities as these parties have grown in popularity. In certain respects, the bachelorette party is probably a bit easier to plan than the shower, if only because there are few preset conventions to follow.

Pay Up to Party!

Who pays for this shindig, anyway? Once again, it is you and the rest of the bridesmaid troupe who are responsible for footing the bill. Don't empty your savings account to pay for a party that you really can't afford; you are not expected to foot the bill for the bachelorette party by yourself. Instead, ask if everyone will pitch in a little for key costs like the limo rental, hotel rooms, or a stripper. As with the shower, plan a party that fits everyone's budgets.

e✔ Fact

Make sure everyone saves her receipts, then total all the expenses and split the bill evenly after the party. If you are the maid of honor, you may wish to take charge of the financial elements if all the bridesmaids are participating.

You may also ask the partygoers to contribute. For example, if you're planning a ski weekend and you're renting a chalet or condo, ask everyone who comes (bridesmaids and other girlfriends) to chip in for the rental cost and to cover their own individual expenses like lift tickets and so on. If you want to spring for something, bring food and/or drinks that the group can enjoy over the course of the weekend, and split the cost of the bride's lift tickets and other expenses among the bridesmaids.

ⓔ✪ Essential

Often each guest pays her (or his) own way and then everyone chips in to cover the costs for the bride. It is a pretty simple way to keep costs under control on a per-person basis.

There are many elements you can add to a bachelorette party to make it more fun and memorable, including games, decorations, and props. When planning the party, you may wish to delegate one responsibility to each bridesmaid. For instance, one bridesmaid can be in charge of buying props, one in charge of buying cocktails or mixers, and one in charge of organizing games or activities.

Breaking the Bank

Luckily, there are not as many components of a bachelorette party as there are in a wedding . . . but it will still cost you! Here is a list of what you need to consider when preparing the budget for a simple party:

- Beverages/cocktails
- Food
- Game or activity supplies
- Invitations
- Props
- Transportation

Here's the Plan

Now that you have the general idea of the what and why of a bachelorette party, it is time to get planning. The party itself does not have to be big or grandiose, just remember to take the bride's sense of style, expectations, and demeanor into account as you begin the planning.

 Fact

> Everyone's got a different definition of fun. While some brides-to-be may enjoy drinking and dancing 'til 6 A.M., others may prefer a relaxing day at the spa with their closest friends. Be sure to plan something that suits the bride's temperament.

Getting Down to Business

As with the shower, you should enlist the help of the bridesmaids, who will probably be eager to add their two cents to coming events. Once you've decided the tone this event will take, you'll be able to narrow down your options. If you want a more subdued event, for example, you may wish to plan a day on the golf course, an elegant dinner out, or a day of beauty treatments. If you want to plan something a bit wilder, then you may consider hiring a limo, ordering a stripper, or even planning a girls' getaway to Las Vegas. Solicit the opinions of the bridesmaids; they may have some inspiration from other bachelorette parties they've attended.

It is important to keep every guest in mind when planning the big soiree. If much of the crowd doesn't drink, then don't revolve activities solely around drinking games or barhopping. If only a fraction of the group plays golf, then don't plan a day on the links (even if you and the bride happen to love it). Plan something that everyone can enjoy, or risk a party that poops out right from the start.

Options Galore

Bachelorette parties began as a direct response to the bachelor party revelry that men have long enjoyed. Therefore, it's only natural that they originally embraced the same basic tenets—bar- and club-hopping, strippers, and drinking to excess. Some brides thrive on the equality that the bachelorette party brings, and thoroughly enjoy these activities to boot; other brides like the concept of togetherness but would prefer something a bit mellower (and just as much fun). There are additional factors, too, that will contribute to the style of event you throw, most dominant among them being the guest list. While one style of party is perfectly appropriate for your ten sorority sisters, the same party may make the mother and aunt of the bride extremely uncomfortable.

🅔❗ Alert

When planning the bachelorette party, definitely follow the bride's wishes. Don't force an evening of wild drinking and partying if she doesn't want it.

If a night on the town isn't right for your bride, there are options. Following are a few ideas:

BACHELORETTE PARTY OPTIONS:
- Spa day or weekend
- Wine tasting
- Comedy night

- Concert
- Play
- Crafting (such as painting pottery or scrapbooking)
- Shopping and tea in the city
- Elegant dinner

What's Your Bachelorette's Style?

Very likely, you can guess what tone of event your bride would like, or perhaps she has let her wishes be known. If not, the following quiz is meant to help you determine what style party your bride would prefer.

1. **When the bride's fiancé heads out for a night with the boys, what does the bride usually do?**
   A. Breathe a sigh of relief, get a pint of her favorite ice cream, and settle down for a relaxing night with a new paperback.
   B. Call a friend to enjoy a nice dinner out and a movie.
   C. Get together with a group of girlfriends for a night of bar- and club-hopping 'til 3 A.M.

2. **You're renting a movie with the bride. Which choice best symbolizes her preference?**
   A. Harry Potter or the latest Disney flick
   B. Being John Malkovich or Gosford Park
   C. Basic Instinct or Unfaithful

3. **Which best represents the bride's last vacation?**
   A. A trip to Hilton Head with her parents and little brothers
   B. A weekend at Canyon Ranch with her sister
   C. A trip to Hedonism with her girlfriends

4. **When the bride talks about a "wild time," what is she referring to?**
   A. A few glasses of wine during happy hour with her sister
   B. Drinking, dancing, and flirting at a hot new club
   C. Skinnydipping in a hot tub with two hot guys she just met

5. **What best represents the bride's fashion sense?**
   A. Ann Taylor
   B. Bebe
   C. Frankie B

If your answers were mostly A: This girl tends to be more wholesome and conservative. Not much for the bar scene, this girl is probably more comfortable with a quiet evening of baby-sitting than with a wild night on the town. Tread carefully when incorporating the racier aspects of the bachelorette party—even though it's a special evening, things like sexual props, daring games, and strippers may make her very uncomfortable. On the other hand, she may be waiting for a night like this to come out of her shell, so don't automatically assume that she wants kid stuff for her bachelorette, either. Your best bet? Feel her out and see what her bachelorette tolerance level is.

If your answers were mostly B: More of a sophisticate, this girl has been known to get her groove on, in a cool, classy way. While she may not enjoy wearing a buck-a-bite candy neck-lace for slobbering guys to pounce on, she will probably enjoy a night of good eats and upscale barhopping. Reservations at your city's hardest-to-get-into restaurant, followed by martinis at the hottest club, will do this bride-to-be just fine.

If your answers were mostly C: For this bride, who puts the phrase "Been there, done that" to shame, you'll really need to get creative. This bride is sure to be satisfied with an out-of-towner where she can let it all hang out before the big day. A happening venue like New Orleans, Las Vegas, or New York might do the trick. Then again, you may be surprised, she may be through sowing her wild oats and prefer a quieter gathering of her closest girlfriends. Definitely check with this wild child to determine her ultimate wishes.

Who's Who

Who is the hostess or hostesses? Who do you invite? Is it okay for the bride's mother to attend? You'll need to pin down your guest list first; the list, not just in size, but by inclusion, will affect the type of party you plan. After all, you don't want to hire the stripper, rent the limo, and stock the bar only to discover that the bride's future mother-in-law will be in attendance. Then again, the bride's future mother-in-law may be young at heart and ready for a wild night of her own, so everything ultimately depends on the personalities of those involved.

Playing Hostess

Someone has to be in charge. Someone has to lead the group. Who is that, you may ask? This responsibility falls upon you and the rest of the bridesmaids in the party. The brides-maids, typically led by the maid of honor, act as hostesses of the bachelorette party. It is their responsibility to plan, budget for, invite, and entertain—or at least schedule entertainment for—the guests.

Size Matters

One bride envisions a simple girls' night, complete with wine, Chinese take-out, pedicures, and late night chats with five or six of her closest girlfriends. Another bride has dreams of a giant bash before her wedding with all her women friends in attendance—her philosophy has always been the more, the merrier. A house party with fifty guests, cocktails, and the requisite male stripper is in order. Both scenarios have their issues and complications. So how do you determine the guest list for this once-in-a-lifetime shindig?

 Fact

Like the bridal shower, the bachelorette party planning and hosting duties should be delegated among the bridesmaids. So, too, should the cost. Have each bridesmaid save her receipts, then add up everyone's costs and split them among the bridesmaids after the party.

The Guest List

The guest list should definitely be determined with the help of the bride. In general, bachelorette parties can range from a small group of five women to a much larger group of twenty to thirty and beyond! This all depends on your bride's particular circumstances and wishes. If she has a wide social circle and relatively open-minded relatives (and relatives-to-be), the bride may wish to include everyone.

Your best bet when making out the guest list is to assume nothing and to talk to the bride about her expectations. She may also appreciate your input and advice. Be considerate, too. If the bride wants her mother or future mother-in-law to be a part of the event, consider inviting everyone to a dinner or cocktails to include them. You can always make other, possibly more risqué, plans for after.

No matter how large or small the party will be, the following checklist will help ensure you don't forget to consider any important guests:

- ❏ All bridesmaids
- ❏ Bride's sisters
- ❏ Bride's cousins
- ❏ Bride's mother
- ❏ Bride's aunts
- ❏ Bride's future sisters-in-law
- ❏ Bride's future mother-in-law
- ❏ Any other of the bride's future in-laws
- ❏ Bride's childhood friends
- ❏ Bride's high school friends
- ❏ Bride's college friends
- ❏ Bride's coworkers
- ❏ Wives/girlfriends of groom's close friends
- ❏ Men (see below)

Not Just for Girls

Another bachelorette party option may include merging the girls with the boys—creating one all-encompassing bachelor and bachelorette party. Obviously, not every bride and groom will go for this idea, but in recent years it's become more and more common for the party to be coed, or for the two parties to meet up and become one at a certain point in the evening. Maybe your group of friends isn't big on separating by gender, or the bride has a lot of male friends she wouldn't want to exclude from her celebration. Whatever the reason, the bachelorette/

bachelor party is another opportunity to celebrate a fun evening (or day) with everyone involved in the wedding.

Parties to Remember

Once the guest list is established, be sure to send out invitations at least six weeks before the party date to ensure guests, especially those from out of town, have time to make the proper arrangements. Unlike showers, bachelorette party invitations are a bit more lax, with plans and invitations often traveling by phone call, word of mouth, or e-mail. The more formal the event, the more formal your invitation should be.

Out on the Town

Now that you've narrowed down your bride's style, you've got a decent idea of the tone this party will take, and you've decided you'll definitely be heading out on the town. But there are still lots of options that range from racy to respectable, and besides, who says the bachelorette party can't be both? The following are some ideas for specific theme parties that will take you outside the comforts of home. Take these ideas and follow them exactly, or give them your own unique spin to make them completely original.

Big Night Out

This event is perfect for both the bride-to-be who doesn't get out with the girls very often and the one who can't get enough fun with her friends. The Big Night Out can be planned with many variations, but here's one that's universally fun.

Meet at one central place, like a bridesmaid's home or apartment. Have a few cocktails and munchies and play a warm-up game or two. Embark in your limousine, which you've hired in advance to escort your group anywhere it wants to go. (Develop a flexible itinerary ahead of time, so you'll have some consensus and/or ideas of where you want to go before the limo driver starts asking for destinations.) Pick at least one destination that's a bit of a drive, just so you can actually spend some time enjoying the limo before you start bar- and/or club-hopping.

Be sure to have some snacks on hand in the limo to absorb what will presumably be a great deal of alcohol. Take advantage of games for the "outside world," also detailed later in this chapter. If you're feeling daring, escort the bride to a strip club for her last live glimpse at a naked stranger.

🅔✔ Fact

Props and games always make the big night out more fun (and will identify you immediately as a roaming bachelorette party). Read on for ideas for bachelorette party activities, games, and novelties.

If you split the cost of the limo, the munchies, and the bar or club cover charges among all the bridesmaids—or even better, among all the attendees—this bachelorette party shouldn't cost a great deal of money. Obviously, the more attendees, the cheaper the night, but don't overstuff your limo, or you'll be very uncomfortable. You also have to take into account where you are holding the event—a big city soiree is more costly than a small town buffet!

A Sophisticated Dinner

What woman doesn't love the opportunity to try a great new restaurant? And there's no better excuse to splurge than a friend's or family member's bachelorette party. For this party, pick a restaurant that has very good food and an even better atmosphere; that is, don't pick a place that's too formal or stuffy, or you might risk attracting the ire of the entire restaurant as the girls start to let loose.

To avoid this unwelcome complication, choose a lively, happening restaurant with lots of young people and an understanding wait staff, and you'll be all set. Keep the wine and cocktails flowing, and hope for a waiter who'll willingly accept a little friendly banter throughout the meal. If you wish, have a limo (or a designated driver) take the group to a bar or club afterward to dance off that delicious and decadent dinner.

🄴❗ Alert

If you're going out to dinner, try to get reservations in your city's hottest, most happening restaurant. Call well in advance so you're sure to secure a spot. Be sure to let them know it is a party!

The individual price per person at a group dinner always seems higher than at a dinner for two, probably because there are no holds barred when it comes to ordering appetizers for the table, keeping the drinks flowing, and ordering plenty of desserts and extras to share. This said, prepare to drop a little money on this evening, particularly if you'll be heading out afterward for more drinks and dancing or if you've hired a limo. The nice dinner out, after you've all split and added in the bride's expenses, too, will probably cost you at least a hundred bucks.

Comedy Club

A variation of the Big Night Out, this party idea makes the comedy club the focal event of the evening. If your group loves to laugh and you know there are some quality clubs in town, this may be an ideal pick for you. Of course, it may also be another limo stop on the Big Night Out circuit, as well.

Keep in mind that many comedy clubs have cover charges and/or two-drink minimums, so call ahead to see if they'll offer your group a break or a special group rate. Be sure to let the comedians on stage know why you're there. Very likely, the bride will become the center of some good-natured ribbing.

Every comedy club works differently. Call ahead, or check out your local clubs' websites to get the scoop on costs. Be sure to call in advance to negotiate group rates and also to reserve enough seats to accommodate your group.

There's No Place Like Home

While painting the town is always fun, sometimes there's nothing like the comfort of home. Throwing a home-based party can be an especially good option if there are a lot of guests coming in from out of town; without all the distractions of being out, you'll have more time to actually spend together, either catching up or getting to know one another. There are countless variations on the home party, if you get creative. So read on to discover if the home fires will be keeping you warm this bachelorette party season.

House Party

Like any house party you'd throw, this event can take on countless variations. The bare bones of this shindig, however, involve food, drinks, and some sort of entertainment. But aside from that, this house party can range from relaxed to raving. Typically, this party would be hosted by one of the bridesmaids, with help from the others. You'll definitely want to prepare some food, which can range from a full dinner for a small crowd (if you're especially talented in the kitchen) to easy appetizers and munchies for a larger crowd. To make it even simpler, order pizza or take-out, for which everyone can chip in.

Depending on how ambitious (and understanding) you are, the house party can range from a small group (five to eight guests) to a much larger one (twenty guests or more). In fact, the house party is probably the best way to go if there's a large group of invited guests, only because coordinating a night of limos, dinner out, and barhopping can become a logistical nightmare for groups of more than ten. But that doesn't mean you'll have any less fun; just bring the entertainment in-house, with games, props, and even a palm reader or male stripper or two to keep guests lively and having fun.

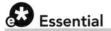 **Essential**

When planning the bachelorette party, put one bridesmaid in charge of each task. Tasks might include food, alcohol, games, decorations/props, transportation, and other "entertainment" (wink, wink).

Of course, you can also give your party a theme to infuse some more character. A South-of-the-Border theme, for instance, would allow you to serve Mexican goodies like quesadillas, nachos, bean dips, and guacamole. It's also always fun to make blender drinks like frozen margaritas with the girls, especially when everyone's pitching in. Another concept for a house party might include a wine-tasting theme, an idea to give the standard house party a more upscale edge (at least until everyone's buzz kicks in). Get a number of bottles of wines to test, both red and white; a good estimate is at least one bottle per person. Have plenty of water and plain crackers on hand to clean the palate in between tastings, and serve wine-friendly foods like fresh shellfish, a variety of cheeses, fruits, and crudités for guests to nibble on. Give each guest paper and pencil to write down their thoughts about each wine, and then compare them at the end. Give the bride a few bottles of wine as a special bachelorette party gift and remembrance.

Another in-house idea might include a decadence theme. The decadence theme is simply an excuse to indulge all the senses, girl-style. For this party, you'd serve champagne and wine, a variety of good chocolates, and a full variety of sweet treats like chocolate-covered strawberries, éclairs, *petit fours*, cheesecakes—all the forbidden, decadent treats that are hard to resist. You might highlight this party by giving "forbidden" gifts to the bride as well, such as lingerie, erotic books, sex toys, or other bawdy gifts you couldn't bring yourself to present at the shower. Top the night off with a romantic or racy chick flick you can enjoy as you all digest your delicious, rich snacks.

 Question

Do I have to give the bride a gift at her bachelorette party?
No, you do not have to give the bride another gift. However, you may wish to give the bride a gag gift or two of bachelorette-related items—these are hard to resist! Go online to find countless fun and goofy bachelorette gifts.

The cost of the house party can range depending on the food and alcohol you serve, and how elaborate you choose to get with favors, gifts, and decorations. However, with everyone pitching in, this is probably the least expensive route to go, even if you decide to serve lobster tails to fifteen guests. Of course, if you order a stripper (another decadent option) it will up the ante by $200 or more, but split among say, ten people, it's only an extra $15 to $25. And won't the look on the bride's face as this studly man gives her his undivided attention be completely priceless, anyway?

The Throwback Slumber Party

Unlike other house parties that may end around midnight, that's the time the slumber party just gets going! Like slumber parties of yore, the primary activities of this party are to stay up all night, giggle, and confess all your pent-up secrets. You may wish to keep this party relatively small to better accommodate a stroll down memory lane.

e☀ Essential

A house party can be a cost-effective alternative to a night on the town. Plus, you can get as creative as you like with the theme, food, decorations, games, or other forms of entertainment.

For example, if you invite the bride's closest friends from high school, be sure to bring out the old photos and yearbooks and relive those seemingly long-lost glory days. Ask all the guests/bridesmaids to raid their closets for anything they might have saved from those days—old notes, love letters, teen magazines, anything they're willing to share with the group.

For eats, have plenty of foods on hand that you regularly scarfed down during your teenage years—tortilla chips, cheese dip, microwave pizza bagels and mozzarella sticks, popcorn, and soda. Of course, now that you're of age, you can actually add alcohol to this gathering legally, and you won't have to spend half the night strategizing how and where you're going to get it.

On one hand, this party is about as low cost as you can get. Your biggest expense might be a pizza or a case of wine. On the other hand, you could go all out and make it a fancy slumber party with champagne and gourmet cheeses. Whichever way you go, ultimately, you'll be able to spend some genuine quality time together.

Poker Night

Again, why should the boys have all the fun? Poker night is a perfect way for the girls to get together, bond, and win a little cash. To properly host poker night, be sure to have a number of round tables that seat four to five people; plenty of decks of cards (get some naked-man playing cards to stay in theme); poker chips that guests can "purchase" when they arrive; cigars and cigarettes to create the requisite smoky atmosphere; and plenty of good beer and single-malt scotch to smooth out the rough edges.

Don't forget some music in the background and some tasty munchies for what's sure to be a long, fun evening. You may also wish to run a fifty/fifty split raffle. To do this, sell tickets for a couple bucks apiece (double-sided tickets that are sold on long rolls are perfect). At the end of the night, pick a ticket: The winner gets half the proceeds of the ticket sales and the bride gets the other half.

Poker night is a comparatively cheap evening, especially if you don't have a losing streak. Of course, you can organize poker night with fake money, allocating a certain number of chips per guest as they come in, or you can gamble with real money, charging, say, $1 per chip. The only other expense will be munchies, drinks, and those naked-man playing cards, which you wouldn't dream of doing without.

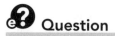 Question

We'd love to do poker night, but not everyone plays. What should we do?
If not everyone is a poker shark (a likely scenario), hire a poker instructor to give a quick lesson at the beginning of the party. Then, make poker night an excuse for a semi-regular girls' night out.

Coed Party

Though a coed bachelorette party may seem a paradox, it's possible to combine the sexes for a night of fun and prenuptial mayhem. There are certain cases when this might make sense for your group. Perhaps you have a social group that's very mixed, and the bride would miss having her close male friends around; or perhaps the bride and groom have decided they'd rather combine their bachelor and bachelorette parties into one big, fun event. Maybe the bride and groom are fundamentally opposed to separating groups based solely on gender.

Plan this party as you would any other party. Perhaps it's a theme party (James Bond masquerade party, Mexican fiesta theme), a simple house party, or renting a room at a local restaurant or bar. Feel free to use any of the bachelorette party ideas in this chapter—just add boys! Some would say the highest cost would be the loss of a girls-only get-together, but if the bride doesn't want to exclude anyone or if she'd prefer joining forces, hey, the more the merrier.

Whatever the reason, it's easy to include everyone in parties like Big Night Out, a sports-related party, or a house party. Even a throwback slumber party would have a whole new dimension with the addition of boys . . . bring your cutest PJs!

The Weekend Getaway

The weekend getaway doubles as a mini vacation for all the guests. It can be a great way to spend relaxed time together without constant distractions. The weekend (or long weekend) getaway might take you anywhere. Good bachelorette party destinations might be a condo in a ski town; an all-inclusive tropical resort such as Club Med; a stylish new hotel and casino (they're popping up all over); or a weekend of pampering at a spa.

🅔❗ Alert

If you know most of the bridesmaids and potential guests are strapped for cash, don't push the idea of a weekend getaway for a bachelorette party. There are plenty of fun things you can still do close to home.

No matter what destination you ultimately choose, take some time beforehand to organize a flexible itinerary so the weekend will have some structure. For example, if you're staying at a ski resort condo, perhaps Saturday and Sunday morning and afternoon will be reserved for ski time, while Friday night you'll head out on the town, and Saturday evening you'll put together a homemade feast and play board games at the condo.

No matter where you go, weekend getaways offer the time and means to relax and spend quality bonding time together before the big day.

A weekend getaway is probably the costliest alternative for a bachelorette party, due to travel costs, accommodations, and incidental costs. Of course, there are always methods to cut those costs, like going to a destination that's within driving distance, sharing the cost of a condo or rental unit among the group, and bringing food and drinks with you.

 Fact

If you're planning a golf outing for a group that includes nongolfers, choose a shorter, executive-style course or a par-three course. These courses generally host less experienced golfers who won't get too frustrated as you go for your tenth shot on a par-three hole. Be sure to have lessons available, as well.

Obviously, a trip to Club Med will cost more than a weekend camping trip, so if you think that many of those on your invite list can't swing it, you may wish to plan something within easier financial reach. Most likely, the bride would prefer to include as many of her close friends as possible and stick closer to home than to plan some elaborate getaway that only two of her friends can attend.

The Sports-Related Event

Why should those fun, all-day golf outings be reserved for just the bachelors? Even if all the girls aren't great golfers, getting out on the course for a day of doffing—or some other fitness-related event—will afford you the outdoors, sun, snacks, and togetherness that the boys have long enjoyed.

Your options certainly aren't limited to golf. Perhaps you'd rather organize an informal tennis tournament followed by a beach barbecue or a bike trip to a scenic destination where you can all enjoy a picnic. No matter what the bride's favorite sport or activity, you can definitely turn it into an excuse for an outdoors bachelorette party that's a unique and healthful alternative to the drinking and barhopping event. It's always possible, too, that your sporting ways may just be a precursor to less health-minded evening activities—why should the fun stop if your group doesn't want it to?

If it's a golf outing, fees can range from $30 to $50 or more per person, depending on the course. If you plan a tennis tournament, hike, or bike trip, the only cost you'll likely have will be for food and drinks. So comparatively, this type of outing will be healthful for your heart—and your wallet.

CHAPTER 7

It's All Fun and Games

Games have long been a part of bridal showers and bachelorette parties. While the traditional games are still popular, today's games are creative and unique. These games run the gamut from the sweet and simple homemaker to the downright personal to the risqué night on the town theme. At the end of the day, the games are all about having a good time, and as a bridesmaid, it helps to know what the expectations are and what's appropriate when incorporating games and activities into these bridal soirees.

Are You a Player?

Games are a good way for guests to interact and enjoy themselves, but they are by no means mandatory. The games should reflect the tone and theme of the shower. Shower games can range from corny to goofy to, believe it or not, somewhat sophisticated. Women seem to fall on either end of the spectrum when it comes to their feelings about shower games. Some women can't tolerate them and dread the moment they begin, while other women wouldn't consider it a proper shower without them.

Essential

Games can often serve as icebreakers, fostering interaction among guests who don't know each other, or they can just serve as a fun diversion between eating and gift opening.

What's the Game Plan?

The most important thing to remember when planning bridal shower games is to tailor them to the group at hand. Don't choose a game that requires guests to bare their souls if you know you have a conservative group. Choose games that are appropriate for your group's general demographics—young, old, mixed, coed. For instance, not many men would enjoy the spice game, where guests guess which spice is which. Keep this in mind and, hopefully, everyone will be enthusiastic. You also need to be careful; there is a fine line when it comes to how much is too much. On average, two to four games during a shower are usually appropriate; any more than that and your guests may start to lose interest.

 **Essential**

Remember to have plenty of supplies on hand. For example, if your games involve writing or list making, have pens and paper on hand as well as firm surfaces on which to write if guests aren't seated at tables (magazines usually do the trick).

We Have a Winner

Prizes are a great way to get guests involved and enthusiastic about playing shower games. For some, this is the reason for playing . . . watch out for the competition, ladies! Your best bet is to offer the winners small gifts that will have universal appeal. You may also wish to include one grand prize, such as a bottle of wine or champagne, a gift certificate for a pedicure or manicure, a basket of lotions and shampoos, or another item you think your guests might like. The following list has a few ideas you can use to reward the participants.

WINNING IDEAS

- Aromatherapy soaps
- Bubble bath/bath oils
- Candles
- Candy/chocolate
- Coasters
- Coffee/tea mugs
- Flowers/plants
- Gift cards (for coffee, spa treatments, etc.)
- Hand lotion
- Kitchen gadgets/trinkets
- Photo albums/frames

- Small bottle of perfume
- Tea/coffee
- Stationery

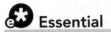 **Essential**

Don't forget to have a couple of extra prizes on hand. There could always be a tie . . . and you never know, Aunt Martha and your college pal Amy could get into it over some fancy soap.

Game Time

There are countless options for bridal shower games. Some are old, some new, and some traditional. Heck, you can even create your own—it is all up to you! Some of the following ideas may be familiar to you; in fact, you may have played them before. Remember, choose the games you feel your particular group will be enthusiastic about playing. Ask each bridesmaid to be in charge of a game (gathering supplies and explaining the details to the guests) to keep them running smoothly.

Whatcha Playing?

Before jumping right into all the details of the games, you need to think about the crowd, theme, and variety of games you want to play at the shower. You must also take into account how much space you have to play in, as some games require moving around, and if there isn't much room to do so, the game will be a flop. Here's the scoop on long-favored games.

The Name Game

This is a simple, quiet game guests can play throughout the shower. At the top of a piece of paper, write the bride's and groom's names—for instance, Kimberly and Scott. The guest who creates the most new words using the letters of the names wins. For example, words derived from these two names would include "kilt," "bet," "best," or "toy."

Wedding Song

As each guest enters, supply her with a small sheet of paper to jot down her wedding song (or her favorite song with a boyfriend, if she's not married). Later in the party, have the bride announce each of the songs that have been written down; guests then guess whom each song belongs to. The person with the most correct guesses wins—bonus points if she guesses what song the bride and groom have chosen. This is a fun way of discovering the wedding songs of family and friends, especially of older guests.

Bridal Bingo

This game takes a little advance prep work, but it's a fun diversion during the gift-opening session. To play bridal bingo, give each guest a customized bingo card (for fun, write the letters B-R-I-D-E or M-A-R-R-Y at the top). In each square, write the name of a popular shower gift. These might include blender, plate, pitcher, cheese grater, toaster, lingerie, colander, frying pan, spatula, pillowcases, bath towels, and so on. (Have all the bridesmaids chip in to make these cards, as it can be a bit time consuming.)

As the bride opens a gift that matches an item in the bingo square, the guest can cover it or cross it off. When she gets five in a row, she yells, "Bingo!" and wins a prize. Much fanfare can be made of checking her numbers against the gifts already opened. And like regular bingo, you can continue playing the game until someone covers four corners, the inside square, or her whole card.

Spice Girls

This is a fun game for all ages, and would make a great tie-in to a kitchen theme shower. Take about ten spices and cover the labels with the letters A through J. Then pass them around and ask guests to identify each spice. Have them write their answers on a sheet of paper, indicating each spice by its letter. At the end of the game, reveal the spices. The guest with the most correct matches wins.

 Fact

A super simple game is called "The Right Date." It requires very little preparation or supplies; just ask all of the guests for the date of their wedding anniversary (or birthday for single guests). Whoever has a date that comes closest to the wedding date wins a prize.

Safety-Pin Game

This is a silly game that will keep guests on their toes. Give each guest a safety pin when they arrive to pin to their shirt. Then pick a word that you think will be used fairly often at the shower, such as "bride," "groom," or "wedding." Tell the guests that this word is off-limits over the course of the shower. If a guest is caught using it, whoever caught her can take her safety pin. Maybe she has already collected a safety pin or more from other loose-tongued guests; if so, she has to give up all the pins she's collected in addition to her own. Whoever collects the most safety pins by the end of the shower is the winner.

Purse Game

At various intervals during the gift-opening session, one of the bridesmaids will act as emcee, announcing to guests that they'll be playing the purse game. The bridesmaid will then announce random items, and if a guest happens to have that item in her purse, she wins a prize. The more obscure the item, the bigger and better the prize. It's a funny way to see what women will actually schlep around in their purses. Try items like underwear, sugar packets, foreign currency, condoms—whatever you think would be fun and appropriate for your particular group.

 **Essential**

> Be sure to have someone be responsible for taking photos; this is surely an event the bride will want to relive later. Also, be sure to get shots of the set up and all the pretty things you have done for the bride.

Guess the Goodies

Fill a large decorative jar with white or colored candied almonds. Ask the guests to figure out how many almonds are in the jar. They can take as long as they want; at the end of the shower, ask them to hand in their answers on a slip of paper. The person who comes closest to the number wins the jar and the almonds. (Feel free to substitute another type of candy or perhaps the bride's or groom's favorite candy.)

Mish-Mash Marriage

Scramble the letters in words associated with love and marriage: kiss (siks), love (voel), garter (tergar), and so on. Set a time limit for the guests to figure out the scrambles. The one who completes the most wins.

Famous Couple Trivia

Develop some trivia questions with a love theme for your shower. Sample questions can be:

- What pop princess, who got hitched on a whim in Las Vegas, had a marriage that lasted only 55 hours? (Answer: Britney Spears)
- *Dawson's Creek* meets *Top Gun*. What famous couple married at a castle in Italy? Bonus points: What was/is their tabloid nickname? (Answer: Tom Cruise and Katie Holmes; Tom-Kat)
- Who were Lucy and Ricky Ricardo's best friends? (Answer: Fred and Ethel Mertz)

Memory Game

After the bride-to-be has opened all of her gifts, ask her to leave the room for a few minutes. Pass out pencils and paper to the guests, and ask them to answer questions about her: What is she wearing? What color are her shoes? Does she have nail polish on? Is she wearing earrings? What is her middle name? And any other questions you can think of. The guest with the most correct answers wins a prize.

Pin It on the Groom

If your live groom is unwilling to volunteer his services, draw the silhouette of a man on a large piece of paper. Attach a photo of the groom's face to the top. Blindfold the guests, spin them, and have them attempt to pin a flower on his lapel.

Mummy Bride

This is a fun and creative game to get people up and moving. Have the ladies divide into teams of three or four. On each team, one lady is the bride. The other gals get rolls of toilet paper and design a one-of-a-kind bridal gown out of TP. It is silly and funny! The bride acts as the judge as the mummy brides present a fashion show for her.

e✔ Fact

If you are playing games and groups of people win, be sure to have enough prizes on hand for all of the winners; better yet, make it the same prize.

No-Game Zone

Even after being tantalized by all of these fun games, there are instances where games just do not work. The bride may despise them . . . or maybe all of the bridesmaids do. Perhaps the locale doesn't offer enough space or privacy to play games or the ladies are all close friends who rarely see each other and they would prefer to just chat and catch up. Whatever the case, realize it is okay. Nowhere does it say you must play games. Just be sure to have the event move swiftly so there is little lag time and no one gets bored.

Welcome Diversions

Not all shower activities must be games. Of course, there's no specific formula you need to stick to when hosting a shower, but you can put personal touches on traditional aspects of the shower to kick things up a notch. From practical to sentimental, added shower activities can really help reflect the true meaning behind the shower and the coming wedding. They can also help guests connect in a whole new way.

The following are a few ideas to get you thinking about additional activities for your shower.

Create a Scrapbook

Who wouldn't love a scrapbook album with mementos and thoughts from one's closest friends and family members? This is a gift the bride will keep and treasure forever, and guests will enjoy looking at all the pages of memories from fellow friends and family members.

 Fact

> A special shower activity can be inspiring and help connect guests to one another. Choose something that allows guests to reflect on the meaning of marriage or that brings up personal memories of the bride.

Making a scrapbook for the bride involves a small investment in guests' time before the shower. Along with the shower invitation, send a blank page from a scrapbook or photo album. Invite each guest to design a page for the bride using pictures, poems, artwork—anything goes. It should simply reflect the guest's feelings or relationship with the bride. The guest should then bring the page to the shower to add it to an album, which will be presented to the bride as she opens her gifts. (This is best done as a surprise.)

Bridal Quiz Show

The bridal quiz show begins by giving guests a page with questions about the bride, to which the bride has supplied answers (to you only) prior to the shower. You can ask questions from all facets of the bride's life, such as the name of her first pet; the name of her first boyfriend; her major in college; her most embarrassing moment; her proudest moment; the thing she loves most about the groom.

eⅤ Fact

The bridal quiz show is a great way to catch up with the bride while providing a little competition for the guests. It also provides a forum to test the groom's knowledge—like a mini Newlywed Game!

When guests are finished completing questions, one bridesmaid can announce the answers. For added fun, give the quiz to the groom before the shower and read his answers aloud, along with the bride's, to see how much he really knows about his beloved. Undoubtedly, his input will make for a good laugh or two. The person with the most correct answers can be given a prize or memento.

What Makes a Good Marriage?

As guests arrive, give them a sheet of paper and a pen and ask them to share one tip about what they feel makes a good marriage. Then, as a break from opening gifts, have the bride read these tips aloud to the group. For added fun, have the group guess who wrote each individual tip. Inevitably, you will get a full range of ideas, from silly to sentimental. But no matter what the advice, it's a game that really brings to light the meaning of the bridal shower—and reminds the remaining guests of what marriage is all about.

Funniest Memory

If your group is outgoing or big on laughs, this is a game that aims to please. As guests enter the party, give them a sheet of paper and pen to write down the funniest memory that they share with the bride. Once everyone has written their memory, give them to the bride to look through and read aloud. The bride can then elaborate, relaying the funny story to the group. This activity works especially well if the bride can ham it up and tell a good story. If not, they may fall flat and make her uncomfortable—this is not for the shy bride!

 Alert

If your game or activity involves digging up a past memory or creating something unique, be sure to give the guests enough notice and a heads up in the invitation so that everyone can participate and have an enjoyable experience.

Double Duty

Sometimes the best activity can do double duty—it has a role as a shower game and activity. If there's a particularly creative or clever bridesmaid, she may be able to take charge of this one. One idea (and there are many more) is to put together a creative basket. A creative basket is a great gift for bridesmaids to give as a supplement to hosting the shower, especially if you've already given the bride gifts at other showers.

Here's a primer on how to play: Buy a bunch of brand-name products from the supermarket, the names of which you can incorporate into a story about the bride and groom. For example, one sentence might go like this: "As the bride waited months and months for her groom to propose, she knew something would have to 'Tide' her over until she'd see that ring 'Sparkle' on her finger. So, she made a 'Dash' for the border for a 'Bold' weekend of fun and excitement in Tijuana with her girlfriends . . . until it 'Dawn'ed on her that she was really much happier with her man."

ⓔ✱ Essential

Designate one bridesmaid to collect the ribbon and bows as the bride opens the gifts. Use a paper plate, tape, and these ribbons to fashion a bouquet. This is the bride's practice bouquet to be used at the rehearsal.

Create a gift basket of all the products used in the story, and then lift them out as you recite the story aloud for the group. It's a clever way to give the bride household items she'll inevitably need, and to tell a fun story that specifically relates to the bride and groom.

Party Like a Bachelorette

Like shower games, bachelorette party games provide a great forum for guests to interact with each other and with the outside world. Whether you're staying in or going out, there are plenty of fun games you can play to commemorate the occasion with true style and lots of laughs. With bachelorette party games, you can often expect a different, slightly risqué—perhaps bordering on raunchy—feel. Of course, there are also options for a more tame evening.

Fun Games for Home

Staying in for the night doesn't mean you cannot have an over-the-top good time. These games will provide some fun, sometimes goofy, and possibly wild diversions.

PIN THE "TAIL" ON THE MAN

- A variation of the classic pin-the-tail game, except this time the tail's in front. For even more fun and frivolity (and if the bride doesn't object), blow up a picture of the groom (clothed, of course) and use him as the target in question, or paste a picture of his face over the model's.

First Kiss

This is a fun girls-only game that works best for relatively small groups. Each guest tells her first-kiss story (presumably from her younger days), followed by her first-kiss story with her current man. The guests then vote on the best first-kiss story from each category.

🅔! Alert

Be sure that the games you select for the bachelorette party are in line with the bride's sensibilities. Be sure to be sensitive to her personality and beliefs when planning games . . . you do not want the bride to feel uncomfortable or embarrassed.

How Well Does the Bride Know the Groom?

Before the bachelorette party, have one of the bridesmaids go on a fact-finding mission to get info from the groom. Questions she asks may range from the innocent (What was your first dog's name? What is your worst pet peeve?) to the relatively risqué

(What's your favorite body part? What's your wildest time with the bride?). At the bachelorette party, the bride is asked to guess the groom's answers to each question. By the end of the quiz, it will become apparent how well the bride really knows her groom.

I Never

This game can be played with or without drinking. Guests sit together in a circle. Each guest goes in turn; with a declaration of something she's never done. For example, the first guest might say, "I've never kissed two guys in one night." Any guest who actually has done this must confess by taking a sip of her drink (or throwing in a poker chip or a penny or any alternate token). The play then proceeds to the right, with the next guest giving a new "I never." This game tends to get racier as it goes on, and it's amazing to find out what your friends will confess to, especially after a few drinks.

Games for the Outside World

So you're taking this party out on the town and are not quite sure what you can do or get away with? Fear not, these games will help your group make many new friends or—at the very least—provide the bride with a little extra attention.

Suck for a Buck

There are plenty of premade kits for this type of activity, but you can also fashion your own. This game involves giving the bride a special T-shirt with Lifesavers or other hard candies attached to it, either with safety pins, sewn on, or stuck on with a swipe of water (the more strategic the candy placement the more titillating the game).

Then, when she is out and about, she (or her friends and bridesmaids) offers passersby the opportunity to take a "suck for a buck." This also works with a candy necklace, if the bride wishes to wear her own outfit. This game is definitely an ice-breaker with the bar crowd!

 Alert

> If you're planning a scavenger hunt and the group will be driving to find the items on their lists, be sure to insist that everyone obeys traffic rules—no crazy driving to get around faster. Also, no drinking until after the hunt is over. Safety first!

Very Daring

At the start of the night, present the bride with a list of dares she must complete by the evening's end. These dares might include tasks that range from the relatively easy to the increasingly difficult. For example, the first task might be telling the group about her first date with her fiancé while the tenth dare might involve getting a pair of men's boxers by the night's end. Other dares might include standing on a chair in a public place and announcing "I'm getting married" five times; doing suggestive (alcoholic) shots, like the famous sex on the beach; or getting the business cards of ten single guys.

Scavenger Hunt

This is a great game for bachelorette parties that are both in and out of the house. For the scavenger hunt, guests are broken up into teams. Each team is given a list of items they need to return to the party with, in a determined amount of time (an hour or two is best). Each item is assigned a point value, with difficult items being awarded a higher score. Items should definitely be bachelorette party related or related to your childhood/

adolescence (sentimental value). The following are some examples in each point category.

1 POINT
A temporary tattoo (applied to one of the team members, of course)
A condom
An X-rated magazine
A fortune cookie
A copy of the bridal registry

5 POINTS
A pair of handcuffs
A poker chip from a casino
A cigar
A deck of naked-man playing cards
An X-rated video
A bridal veil

10 POINTS
An old rotary phone
A pair of the groom's underwear
An eight-track tape
A red lace garter belt

20 POINTS
A Viagra pill
A vibrator
An original Merlin or Simon game

50 POINTS
A male stripper

Playing with Props

For many, the bachelorette party would not be complete without the props geared toward the single gal's last hurrah. In the
last ten years, an entire bachelorette party industry has sprung
up to meet every girl's need for penis straws, naked-man playing cards, and much, much more. Although many of the items
previously required a trip to the (sometimes) seedy adult store
in town, today's bachelorette items are more readily available.
Find them in novelty stores, party supply stores, and easiest of
all, on the Internet.

Let's Decorate!

What's a bachelorette party without some décor of the possibly tacky and salacious sort? And while they are ultimately sillier
than they are salacious (kind of like male strippers), that's pre-
cisely why they're so much fun. Of course, you can have classy
décor as well, or even mix it up.

e✳ Essential

Bachelorette party-inspired props are a fun way to differentiate the occasion from any other night on the town.
Time how long it takes the bartender to notice your penis
earrings or the waiter to spy those penis straws you've sur-
reptitiously placed in your margaritas.

So what should you do with all these props? Perhaps you'd
like to make your dinner for seven a dinner for eight, with your
blowup doll in tow; maybe the bride can show off her Bling-
Bling ring to inquiring parties at the bars. The gummy butts,

gummy penises, and cock candles are the perfect accents to your house party. Get creative. Show off your props with pride.

Consider incorporating some of the following into your bachelorette bash:

- **Penis piñatas**
- **Suck for a Buck T-shirt and candy kit**—everything you need to make the bride a T-shirt that offers passing barflies the opportunity to suck a candy—off her shirt—for a buck (put the proceeds toward blow-job shots)
- **Gummy butts and gummy penises**—for the hungry crowd
- **X-rated fortune cookies**—surprise your friends and family with what's inside
- **Penis-shaped Jell-O shot tray**—makes Jell-O shots even more exciting than usual
- **Pecker earrings**—for the discriminating bachelorette fashionista
- **Bling-Bling 100-carat ring**—almost as big as J. Lo's!
- **Belly jewelry and body glitter**—for the subtler bachelorette
- **Pecker lantern**—lighting the way to the bathroom as you toss your bachelorette party cookies
- **X-rated karaoke microphone**—is it a penis or a microphone cover? Fool your friends!
- **Glow-in-the-dark blowup dolls**—perfect company for the bride when her fiancé doesn't make it home from his own bachelor party
- **Pecker Party Lights**—the perfect decorative complement to Pink Nubby Cock Candles
- **Tantalizing toilet paper**—just try not to get aroused by the naked stick figures pictured here!

Now That's Entertainment!

Entertainment is a key element to the bachelorette party. It may even be the glue that holds the party together. The ladies will be expecting and may even be eager for some form of entertainment—don't worry, the strippers are coming! But before the strippers take over, take a minute or two to consider some other alternatives to the traditional male stripper.

Entertain Me!

As the party planner, don't forget you have choices when it is time to determine the evening's entertainment. The following ideas can be used in lieu of the aforementioned stripper.

- Palm reader
- Tarot card reader
- Astrologist
- At-home party specialist (adult toys, for example)
- Musicians
- Magicians
- Traveling spa party

Adult Entertainment

There's one more important aspect of the party you may want to consider. In fact, some consider it a tradition. Yes, it is time to take it all off, and chat about strippers! Should every bachelorette party include one? No, but if you want one, how do you find him? Again, the bride will probably have a pretty definite opinion about whether or not she'd welcome a male stripper. Obviously, you might want his arrival to be a surprise, so you may wish to do some sleuthing to determine if the bride would approve or not. Obviously, besides the bride's wishes, you'll also need to factor in the guest list when considering a stripper; if it's a large party with in-laws and older generations in attendance, a stripper may not be the best idea.

❓ Question

We want to surprise the bride with a stripper, but we are really not sure how she would feel about this.
Without flat out asking her, tell her a story about a bachelorette party that featured a stripper (make-believe is okay here). If she's against the idea, she'll probably seize the opportunity to let you know. However, if her reaction is, "How fun" or "Was he hot?" it may indicate she's open to the idea.

Where to Look?

The thought of hiring a stripper may fill you with some trepidation. Will you have to go to some seedy strip club to point and pick? Or worse, will you call, give your credit card number, and then wait in vain for someone from the agency to show up, only to find later you've been charged double for nothing?

Luckily, hiring your man is as easy as flipping through the Yellow Pages. While "Strippers" will probably not yield the results you're looking for (too obvious for the phone book people, perhaps), "Entertainment" or "Entertainers" will. Most likely, there will be large display ads as well as the regular listings—hey, this is big business. You're bound to find at least a few appropriate listings right away.

Fact

To avoid a dreaded disaster upon the entertainment's arrival, ask the booking agency if they will allow you to choose your specific stripper by looking through photos. Perhaps they have such a service available online.

Hiring Him

To avoid being put into any compromising position (no pun intended), ask the following questions when hiring your guy:

- **What will this service cost?** Is there one flat rate, or can you order extras à la carte?
- **How long will the performance be?** (That's minutes, not inches.)
- **Will an encore cost more?**
- **What forms of payment are accepted, and when do you have to pay?** (Some services will ask for half in advance and the other half upon completion of services.)
- **Can you see your guy in advance?** Is there a video of him, or a place where you can take a sneak peak at his performing style?
- **Can he wear something specific?** Perhaps you want to goof on the bachelorette by ordering a dancer in doctor garb (her current fiancé's occupation), or in fireman's garb (like her last beau).
- **What if he doesn't show up?** Are you entitled to some sort of refund, and/or is there a backup to take his place?
- **What, exactly, will he do?** Take it all off, strip down to a G-string, what? You should probably be (at least mentally) prepared if he's going to strip down completely.

The Strip Club

Of course, you can skip all the sleuthing by bringing the horse to water, so to speak, and visit a strip club yourselves. If there's one in your town or a nearby destination, going to a strip club will be an event you won't soon forget. Full of whooping, laughing women, the male strip club resembles a comedy club more than a seedy or sexy strip club—aside, of course, from the unclad men.

 Alert

Be sure to treat your stripper with respect. He is simply making a living, and while he may seem as if he's got unflappable confidence when he's standing before you like a modern-day Adonis, that's no reason to insult him or question his choice of occupation.

If you plan to take your bachelorette party to the club instead of ordering "take-out," call the club ahead of time to see if there are any group rates or special rooms your party can take advantage of. Then the bride can pick her favorite from a wide variety of onstage hotties. You're sure to have a blast creating a night that the bride will not soon forget.

CHAPTER 8

Wedding Day Warm-Up

It is coming; can't you feel it? The errand running is kicking into gear. The bride is calling you more often. There are dress fittings to attend, shoes to break in, and manicures to be had! Overall, there is excitement in the air . . . the wedding day is drawing nearer, and while it is work for the bride and her bridesmaids, it is also a great time to be had—a memorable and unique experience that you get to share with a great friend.

Bridesmaids-a-Lunching

Many brides choose to honor the bridesmaids with a traditional bridesmaids' tea or luncheon. This is a fun and intimate gathering of the bride's closest friends. It can be very casual or a little more formal, but mainly it is a time for the bride to celebrate with those closest to her. That being said, there are many brides who do not host a bridesmaids' tea, and no bridesmaid should take this as a slight against them. There is no requirement for this event.

Just the Facts

The bridesmaids' tea, held on the weekend or in the days prior to the wedding, is an opportunity for the bride to show her gratitude to the bridesmaids and treat them to a celebration. This is an event for the bridesmaids only; however, mothers have been known to attend. Very close relatives may also be invited.

🅴❓ Question

Are there any other options for taking the bridesmaids out?
The tea doesn't have to be a tea in the technical sense; it can be any type of event you want it to be. Lunch, a spa day, cocktails and hors d'oeuvres, wine tasting, or dinner are other options.

Not all brides honor the tradition of the bridesmaids' tea—and it is not mandatory—but it can be a nice, relaxing event that gathers the bridesmaids together one last time before the wedding actually occurs. It's often held at a restaurant or the bride's or her mother's home, and is meant to honor the bridesmaids and to show the bride's appreciation for all her maids have done.

What to Do

For the bridesmaids' luncheon, you have no duties except to attend, enjoy, and accept the bride's thanks graciously. The bride often uses this opportunity to present her bridesmaids with traditional small gifts as thanks. These gifts might consist of items ranging from jewelry or handbags to be worn with the bridesmaid dresses; picture frames or albums; small keepsakes such as elegant key rings or hand-sized mirrors; or practical yet pretty gifts such as personalized stationery.

Let's Practice

After all of her planning and preparation, of course the bride wants everything to flow smoothly on her wedding day. A well-orchestrated, well-planned rehearsal is the key to success. Usually the night before the wedding, all involved parties gather at the ceremony site so they can familiarize themselves with the venue and participate in a quick run-through of the ceremony. Afterward, it is off to a fun and relaxing evening at the rehearsal dinner.

Down the Aisle We Go

Most ceremony rehearsals are held one to two days before the wedding, at which the bride, groom, parents, and the wedding party can learn exactly where they need to be and what they need to do at the ceremony. Most weddings have slight style variations, so this rehearsal time can prove extremely valuable. For example, some officiates will direct groomsmen to meet the bridesmaids before they reach the end of the aisle, while others may direct groomsmen to hold their places near the groom until the end of the ceremony.

There are many more small, seemingly inconsequential details that you'll review, and these will become absolutely vital as hundreds of eyes fall on you during the actual ceremony. Thus, the rehearsal is a valuable time to pay attention and do what you're told, so try to save your daydreams about that incredibly gorgeous groomsman for later.

Essential

Be sure to bring the ribbon and bow bouquet from the bridal shower to the rehearsal. The bride can practice holding and passing it off to the maid of honor. If there is no bouquet, grab a bunch of silk flowers.

Personal Rehearsal Assistant

At the rehearsal, all of this planning suddenly becomes very real. The bride is the center of attention and has so much to do and think about; she may even feel like she is being pulled in twenty directions. She may really need help at this time, but be unsure how to ask for it.

There is no doubt there are a lot of items to pack up and transport to various locations prior to the wedding day. Ask the bride if she could use some assistance organizing these items and getting them to their final destinations. Even one less drop off could be a huge relief to the bride. Here is a list of items the bride may need to remember:

- Aisle runner
- Fee for officiate
- Fee for site

- Flower girl basket
- Itineraries
- Maps or written directions
- Marriage license
- Practice bouquet
- Ring pillow
- Unity candles
- Wedding-day transportation information
- Wedding programs

Copy Girl

If the bride does not have a wedding planner, she may be responsible for providing copies of the itinerary to the family and wedding party members at the rehearsal. Offer to make those copies for her (once she has finalized the plans) and even help pass them out at the rehearsal.

🎇 Essential

Arrange for the bride and groom to ride to the rehearsal dinner together (perhaps you can act as their personal chauffer). This may be their last alone moment for the next twenty-four hours! The hoopla of planning often leaves little "us" time for the happy couple.

Chauffer

Driving when you are stressed, excited, in a hurry, or simply overwhelmed is never good. If possible, offer to be the bride's chauffer for the rehearsal and possibly the wedding day.

Room Service

Arrange for snacks and drinks to be available in the hotel room (or getting ready location) on the wedding day. A bunch of ladies without a snack or water could prove dangerous!

Turn-Down Service

Arrange with the hotel where the newlyweds will stay on their wedding night to have champagne and a midnight snack delivered to the couple's room. If possible, also have a slice or two of their wedding cake delivered to the room. Chances are they had little time to eat dinner or much more than a bite of the cake.

The Rehearsal Dinner

The rehearsal dinner is a time for the people involved in the wedding to gather and enjoy some special, more intimate time together after the rehearsal and prior to the big day. The rehearsal dinner is the time for personal stories, reminiscing, and toasts. Nothing is required at the rehearsal dinner. Many times the couple will present the attendants and their parents with thank-you gifts, and often there is a round of toasts.

 Fact

The rehearsal dinner is the perfect time for those more personal toasts. Check with the hosts in regards to the schedule, and prepare some special words for the bride and groom.

Generally, the rehearsal dinner is hosted (and paid for) by the groom's parents. The members of the wedding party are expected to attend, but dates are not always a part of the equation when it comes to rehearsal dinner invitations. If you are married, engaged, have been dating someone long term (i.e., a serious relationship), most likely he will be invited as well.

Ways to Help (That She May Not Even Know About)

No doubt, the bride is busy. She has planning and fittings and packing to do. She thinks she has it all under control . . . and she may. However, there are ways a trusty bridesmaid can assist over the course of the last few weeks of planning. In fact, some of these ways she may not even know about. So get going, read ahead, and get ready to be Bridesmaid of the Year!

Alert

Be sure to check with the happy couple before scheduling anything to avoid conflicts. Also, extend an invitation to them, but do not expect their attendance—they will undoubtedly be swamped with wedding details.

Social Director

Out-of-town visitors may wish to fill their time in the hours leading up to the wedding by visiting local landmarks, museums, and galleries. Of course, there is always shopping or just the experience of a leisurely lunch at a great restaurant. However, they may have no idea what to do. Offer to help the bride make arrangements for or provide the guests with information to make their stay comfortable and memorable.

If there are any organized tours scheduled and you are familiar with the area, try to arrange to take part in the activity; the bride may not be able to. As one who is familiar with the area, you can provide directions, local information, and simply help organize the other guests.

✴ Essential

Offer to contact the local chamber of commerce or visitors bureau to get local maps and listings of area attractions for the family, wedding party, and guests. These items are usually provided free of charge and are a great help.

The wedding party may have this same dilemma. If they, like the other guests, are looking for something to do, perhaps you might arrange a little social gathering during the hours leading up to the wedding. You can plan a local golf outing, a relaxing hike, a luncheon, or you might ask the hotel if they'll open up a hospitality suite for you all to hang out in before the wedding begins. It is always more fun when everyone gets to know each other a little better.

Fittings and Shopping

It seems the to-do list is ever growing in the days before the wedding. Most likely, any fittings for the bridesmaids will be done and they will have picked up their dresses by this point; typically, the bride has a final fitting in the last couple of weeks. She may need a special helper on pickup day. It is important to transport the dress correctly and carefully at this point. A friend to help her load the car is invaluable—it is a lot of dress for her to wrangle by herself!

Salon Appointments

At this point, wedding day beauty details should be in place. But what about those extras: a massage, a facial, an eyebrow wax. Use your friend's wedding as a great excuse to treat yourself to a little pampering. Perhaps this even means attending her hair and makeup preview with her. Get together with a friend, and possibly another bridesmaid, or your date, and spoil yourselves for a few hours.

 **Essential**

What girl doesn't love to shop? Well, that may be true, but when you have what seems like a million things on your list, it can be stressful. Grab the bride and take her shopping for those wedding essentials, or even offer to do the shopping for her (if she'll let you).

Right-Hand Gal

As the day draws nearer, it will seem like there is less and less time for the bride to get everything accomplished. What could be better than a bride's own personal right-hand gal? You have done your duties, but these few extra niceties can really make all the difference for a busy bride.

Assembly Line

Offer to help the bride package or prepare the wedding favors. Tying bows or bagging candies are simple yet time-consuming endeavors. It's likely a little help will be appreciated. The same holds true for welcome bags—they do not assemble themselves!

Delivery Person

Welcome gifts (see above) need to be delivered in the days before the wedding, when it seems everything else is happening, too! By this time, the bride should have made the proper arrangements with the hotels, but you can do her a big favor by offering to deliver them to the hotels—a huge help, for sure.

 Alert

> Each hotel has specific requirements for the delivery of welcome gifts—some require a fee, some an exacting list of guest names—so be sure you have all of the necessary information. There is nothing worse than showing up with twenty welcome gifts and no clue what to do.

Tomorrow's Another Day

Offer to gather the bride's dress and take it to her home or the gown cleaners (if she has made prior arrangements), assuming she is leaving right away for the honeymoon. She may also need assistance in getting her bouquet to the preservationist as well, or returning small rental items. Any help you can provide after the event will be appreciated. After all, the bride's job isn't over yet . . . she still has a honeymoon to go on.

Stress Relief

As a bridesmaid, one of your unwritten but integral duties throughout the engagement period is to provide moral support for the bride. At no time will this be more vital, probably, than on the wedding day itself. The bride will inevitably be somewhat nervous in the hours leading up to the wedding ceremony. It's understandable; when you've spent literally hundreds of hours planning and pouring over the details of a one-day event, you tend to invest a lot of yourself in that event's success. Add to that the emotional impact of committing yourself to lifelong marriage, and it's impossible not to feel the pressure.

 **Essential**

> A nervous bride is a natural part of weddings. Do what you can to provide moral support, troubleshooting, and laughter to relieve her wedding-day jitters.

On top of it all, there's the added stress of being on display in front of hundreds of your nearest and dearest, which becomes much more real as the wedding grows closer. Then, there is always the chance, however slight, that the weather does not cooperate, a flight gets canceled, a bridesmaid gets the stomach flu, or the cake shows up very late. Now we are talking real tension.

By providing a mental port for the bride's prewedding storm, you really have an opportunity to show off your bridesmaid skills. While she may not ask for your help outright, utilizing these subtle, behind-the-scenes methods will help you ease her mind—and maybe your own in the process.

Destressing the Bride

When this all becomes a little much for the bride to handle—even if for a moment, and we all have our moments—what can you, dear bridesmaid, do to alleviate her stress and racing thoughts? Try some of the following tactics to help calm the bride's somersaulting stomach in the hours leading up to the biggest commitment she'll ever make. Some of these suggestions are for the days prior to the wedding, and some are for the wedding day, but will need to be prepared or scheduled in advance.

e✔ Fact

Stress need not play a big part in the wedding day, for you or for the bride. By now, all the plans should be in motion, and if they're not, there's nothing you can really do about it anyway. Make an effort to relax and just enjoy the day.

Take Her Out

Grab the bride and treat her to a cup of coffee or a walk along the beach, lake, or in the forest. Give her a chance to get out and refresh and take her mind off of all the planning. Chances are she will come back feeling re-energized.

Make Her Laugh

There's no better tension relief than laughter. Save a humorous anecdote to tell her the day of the wedding, download some of those goofy puns she loves, or relive funny old stories to keep her relaxed. You might even want to download your favorite song from high school or college for a little flashback—it will surely put a smile on her face.

Suggest a Massage or Spa Treatment

A serene spa combined with a skilled technician is the best medicine for easing tension. Suggest to the bride that she schedule a treatment, such as a massage, body wrap, or soothing moisturizing treatment, to relax her. Advise her not to try anything that could adversely react with her skin, like an intense facial or a waxing, too close to the wedding day.

Create an Atmosphere of Calm as You're Getting Ready

Set up aromatherapy candles. Play some light, relaxing music. Dim the lights. Close the door on the chaos of family members, children, or other bridesmaids. Sensory overload can affect even the calmest of brides, so try to tune out the stressful effects of hyper kids, loud music, or overindulgent relatives as the bride attempts to get ready.

Take Charge

She's got enough to worry about just getting ready for this shindig. If she's stressing about the arrival of the photographer, the flowers, and the rest of the bridesmaids, make phone calls on her behalf or delegate some of these organizational tasks. If a wedding-day emergency should arise, try to make as little fuss as possible about it and solve the problem without the bride's involvement. Then help her put on her dress and give her any last-minute beauty touchups.

Provide Water and Snacks

No doubt nerves will prompt the bride to claim she doesn't feel like eating. Whether she's truly too stressed to eat or she's trying to avoid gaining that last extra ounce, it is very important that she has a small meal or a few light snacks (at the very least) in the hours leading up to her wedding. Prepare a snack of healthful fruits and cheese, crackers, or whatever you think she'll be likely to eat so she won't become lightheaded or feel weak as the day goes on. When you get to the reception, bring her a special plate of crudités and hors d'oeuvres during the cocktail hour. She'll be so busy mingling that she won't have the time or inclination to seek them out herself.

Be Her Breathing Coach

The butterflies will surely hit right before she walks down the aisle. To alleviate the physical symptoms, including shaking, a racing heart, or lungs that can't seem to get enough air, advise her to breathe deeply. Like a Lamaze coach, breathe with her and count to ten with deep breaths.

🅴❗ Alert

Food is important, but so is staying hydrated. Be sure to keep plenty of water readily available, especially if it's a hot summer day. Bring straws so she doesn't smudge her lipstick or accidentally spill.

Spare the Details

Don't upset the bride with any bad news. Whether it's bad news from the outside world or something that's gone wrong with a wedding vendor or family member, no good will come of telling her difficult news in the hour before the wedding.

Reassure Her That She Looks Stunning

Tell her she's never looked more beautiful. That she's going to rock her fiancé's world the minute he sees her. Tell her whatever it takes to allay any fears that she looks less than perfect.

Plan for Contingencies

Little things will happen on the day of the wedding—a headache, a run in the stockings, flyaway hair, a chipped nail. A wedding day emergency kit includes simple everyday items as well as wedding-specific items. If the bride has not already prepared an emergency kit, or does not have plans to prepare one, ask her if you can prepare this ever-useful and necessary accessory. Be sure to check with the bride about packing an emergency kit to see if she has special requests. Following is a handy checklist of items to include.

BRIDAL EMERGENCY KIT
- ❏ Aspirin or ibuprofen
- ❏ Baby or talcum powder
- ❏ Bobby pins
- ❏ Wite-Out (last resort for covering up stains on a wedding dress)
- ❏ Bottled water
- ❏ Breath mints
- ❏ Cellophane tape
- ❏ Clean white cloth (for cleaning stains on a wedding dress)
- ❏ Clear bandages or liquid bandage
- ❏ Clear nail polish
- ❏ Corsage pins
- ❏ Crackers, energy bars, etc.
- ❏ Deodorant
- ❏ Double-stick tape
- ❏ Duct tape (one regular and one in white)
- ❏ Extra stockings
- ❏ Facial tissue or handkerchief
- ❏ Glue (super glue, hot glue, and hot glue gun)
- ❏ Hairspray
- ❏ Money
- ❏ Mouthwash
- ❏ Nail glue
- ❏ Nail polish (to match your shade, for a quick touchup)
- ❏ Rubber bands
- ❏ Sanitary napkins/tampons
- ❏ Scissors

❏ Sewing kit (including straight pins, needle, and thread—white and black thread as well as a color to match the bridesmaid's dresses and the groomsmen's accessories)
❏ Spot remover
❏ Static-cling spray
❏ Toothbrush and toothpaste
❏ Tweezers
❏ White chalk (for concealing dirt smudges)

Destressing Yourself

In all of your efforts to calm the bride, you mustn't forget to give yourself a little TLC, too. It's only natural that you, too, may be feeling the pressure of walking down the aisle before hundreds of people you may or may not know, of playing bridesmaid to one of your closest friends, or even to devoting the amount of time and money to this endeavor. To minimize your worries and present a calm, cool, and collected face to the world come time for the ceremony, heed the following advice.

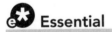 **Essential**

Calm is contagious. While you may be aware of small snafus or may even be feeling anxious yourself, do your best to put on a smile and relax. This feeling of serenity extends to the bride and the others in the room, creating a calm atmosphere.

Do Whatever it is That Helps You Relax

Take a long run or power walk. Do yoga. Read a book. Watch television. Bake cookies. The point is, if you've got extra time on your hands before or on the day of the wedding, avoid stress-causing situations. Don't call your mother if you know you'll end up in an argument. Avoid high-traffic areas of town. Don't pick a fight with your boyfriend if it can wait until Monday.

Prepare in Advance

Don't count on completing any vital tasks on the wedding day. In other words, don't wait until the last minute to do even seemingly quick and easy tasks, like purchasing a pair of pantyhose or pressing your dress. To avoid any last-minute crises, complete all your critical tasks in the days leading up to the wedding. You'll be busy enough without the added complications of a store that's unexpectedly closed or a dress that's stained or damaged from ironing.

Don't Schedule Anything Major on the Day of the Wedding

Try not to venture into situations that might take an unexpected twist, such as driving to an unfamiliar destination or relying on public transportation without a healthy cushion of extra time. You can't control factors like weather and traffic, so it's best to prepare for the worst.

Follow Similar Stress-Relieving Techniques as the Bride

What's good for the bride is good for the bridesmaid! Take a long bath, light a candle, turn on your favorite music, or get a spa treatment. Don't forget to eat something and drink plenty of fluids so you'll have your strength and mental capacity for all the socializing, dancing, and celebrating ahead.

Great Gifts

The wedding day wouldn't be complete without giving a gift to the bride and groom. But what should you get, and how much should you spend? This is a very personal decision. Different regions of the country have different standards of "normal." For example, what's normal in New York City may seem extravagant in the Midwest (and conversely, what's normal in the Midwest may seem cheap in NYC). Of course, anyone who's judging your wedding gift solely by the amount you've spent is materialistic and difficult to satisfy anyway, so the bottom line is this: Give from your heart, and give only what you can afford.

Making the Selection

What should the gift be? A toaster? A blender? A set of silver? A place setting of china? Or something more creative? Obviously, that's up to you. Your only real criterion is to give something you believe the bride and groom will appreciate and find useful.

❓ Question

Do I have to choose a wedding gift from the bridal registry?
No. By choosing something from the registry, however, you'll be sure to give a gift the bride and groom will find useful. But you may also feel compelled to give something more personal and original. Ultimately, the choice is yours.

The first rule of gift-giving is to choose not only what you like, but what you think they'll like. Don't buy them a martini set if they don't drink. Don't give them an ultra-contemporary vase if they prefer classic designs. And if they really just want a lot of practical, everyday items, skip the crystal.

Bridal gift registries can make gift giving simple and stream-lined. Their purpose is to provide gift ideas for the guests, hope-fully in a range of prices to suit various budgets. Be sure to check out the registry and see what the couple has selected. Even if you choose not to purchase a gift from the registry, it may give you direction as to what they need.

Creative Gift Giving

There is the usual assortment of gift ideas, purchased straight from the wedding registry. Of course, the couple will be happy to receive these items; they selected them. However, there are some really creative wedding gift ideas for brides and grooms with all kinds of tastes and interests:

- A piece of art that reflects the ceremony or reception site
- A gift certificate to a great restaurant near their honeymoon destination
- A gift certificate to a home improvement store
- Tickets to an upcoming concert, sporting event, or art exhibit
- Membership to a beer-of-the-month, steak-of-the-month, or other specialty club
- An extravagant item they'll have forever, such as a Tiffany clock, a beautiful crystal bowl, silver chopsticks, etc.
- Something you've made (knit them a blanket, make them a quilt, create a set of pottery—wherever your talents lie)
- A remote car starter (great for cold climates)
- A car CD player
- Hobby-related gifts: ski lift passes to a nearby resort, his and hers tennis rackets, boating accessories, camping gear, three seasons of *The Sopranos* on DVD
- A cool gadget from a specialty store or catalog (Pick out something that you know they'd want but would never get for themselves.)
- A case of wine

- A state-of-the-art bottle opener
- A gift certificate to a local hotel and restaurant for a mini getaway
- His and her massages
- A mailbox for their new home
- A safe (put something fun inside to surprise them)
- A gift certificate for a home cleaning service
- A gift certificate for a special spa treatment, excursion, or meal while on their honeymoon. Call ahead to the hotel to make arrangements.

CHAPTER 9

The Wedding Day

It's the moment everyone has been waiting for. All the buildup, all the planning, and all the celebrations are finally culminating in this moment. While you've most likely attended a wedding or two (or ten), you may never have been a behind-the-scenes player. This is where all the real, down-to-the-wire action is taking place: alongside the bride. Emotions are high, feelings are on the surface, and love is in the air. Ease your anxiety with a primer on what to expect!

And So It Begins

A wedding may only technically be one day, but you may find yourself spending more time getting ready and preparing for the event than you actually spend at the event. As a bridesmaid, you are definitely along for the preparty ride, however long that may be. Even though you're playing supporting actress to the bride's superstar, you will nevertheless experience some of the glow from the spotlight, which means you'll want to be on top of your game.

Essential

Providing the bride with a moment to eat, compose herself, and calmly prepare for the day is a gift that is truly special and greatly appreciated.

Preparing for the Day

The wedding day action typically begins well before the scheduled events. In fact, between the preparation, ceremony, reception, and after hours, a wedding adds up to a very long day. That said, the most important way you can prepare for the day ahead will occur the night before. That's right—it all begins with a good night's sleep.

It may be difficult to heed this advice, particularly if the rehearsal dinner is held the night before the wedding. You may find it disappointing to put a sudden end to the celebration with friends or family you haven't seen in a while, and even harder to get the bride to bid everyone adieu, but if you've got to get up at seven to begin your day, even a professional makeup artist and hair stylist will find it challenging to work with the results of four hours' sleep. And feeling good? Forget about it; you'll be a walking zombie. So what will the day entail, and how can you, beautiful bridesmaid, best get through it?

Wake Up, Sunshine

What better way for a bride to start the morning than with a nutritious breakfast and her favorite morning beverage (coffee, anyone)? The one thing most brides seem to think they can skip on the wedding day is food. Surprise your bride with this early morning treat and start her day, and yours, off right. Be sure to consult with the other ladies of the party, especially if you are not the maid of honor. You should also mention to the bride that you would like to take care of these arrangements, especially if she is the master planner.

 Fact

Go the extra mile for your bride by offering to coordinate the bridal party's wedding-day beauty appointments. It'll be a weight off the bride's mind! This can often be logistically complicated, particularly if bridesmaids are each having more than one service or treatment.

The Salon Experience

A nice tradition that many brides are practicing today is the scheduling of group beauty treatments for the bridesmaids on the morning of the wedding. Sometimes the bride will foot the bill for these treatments as a special wedding-day treat, but she may also expect you to pay for them yourself and/or give you the choice to opt out. If you're on the fence about whether or not to participate, keep in mind that this is a time-honored ritual whose pleasures may come as a surprise—a group of excited and gabby girlfriends, all of whom are being pampered by hired stylists. It's a great time to relax, laugh, and bond a little before the pressures of the day take over.

The bride has probably booked a number of stylists at her favorite salon to provide hair, makeup, manicures, or pedicures. A salon that regularly deals with weddings will understand the complexities of bridal party beauty and should know how to assist you in scheduling and managing appointments accordingly. Ideally, one bridesmaid should be getting a pedicure while another's getting her makeup done while another's getting her hair done, so that you can all cycle around and take full advantage of the time you're at the salon. It's also best to confirm these appointments a week in advance to avoid any wedding day mini tragedies or misunderstandings.

🅔❗ Alert

When it comes to travel and activity in the hours before the wedding, always err on the side of caution. Allot for unexpected traffic delays and give yourself plenty of time to primp, in case of any girl-type disasters.

If you are lucky, the bride will have made arrangements to have the stylists come to her at the hotel or home where she and the wedding party will be getting ready. A traveling hair/makeup/beauty team may seem like a luxury, but when you take into account the fact that no one will have to drive all over town to have these special services done, it is a time and nerve saver. Additionally, these services are competitively priced!

If you're thinking of skipping out of the beauty treatments on the morning of the wedding, remember that this is usually a nice time to relax and unwind before the wedding mayhem actually begins. As much as you may cringe at paying for something you can do yourself, remember that you definitely want to look your best. A month from now, as you look at the bride's photography proofs, you may regret not having your hair or makeup professionally done. And don't underestimate the relief you'll experience by letting someone else worry about getting your hair and makeup perfect.

Down Time

Of course, not every bride will have professional services scheduled for the bridesmaids, or even for herself. Some brides may simply prefer solitude in the hours leading up to the wedding frenzy. Presumably, this will leave you with a lot of down time, especially if the wedding doesn't begin until early evening. What's a fidgety bridesmaid to do, especially if she's from out of town and stuck in a hotel room?

Alert

Even if the bride does not expect the hours prior to the wedding to be filled with salon appointments, do not plan or schedule your regular daily activities—laundry, dog walking, a hike. It is her big day and you never know when she is going to need you.

Even if you anticipate down time, be prepared . . . this is a wedding, after all; things can come up at a moment's notice. However, pack a little kit with some cards, a book, some great magazines—just a few things to entertain yourself and possibly the bride. Don't get too crazy thinking you can sunbathe, but you may be able to fit in a game or some girly chatter over the latest fashions.

Oh, Shoot!

There's no escaping it: Photography is a huge part of the wedding day. If you're lucky, the bride may have knocked off some of the required photos before the ceremony. However, you will still most likely be expected to partake in postceremony photos while everyone else is enjoying cocktail hour. There is nothing you can do about it—it is part of the job—so, smile!

e✱ Essential

A professional wedding photographer will have captured the bulk of the photos prior to the ceremony, and with the wedding party's and family's cooperation, can move the postceremony photo session along nicely so you don't miss a thing—or at least too much!

Smile

At the photo session, the photographer will have a list of formal portraits to take. This list should have been prepared and given to the photographer in advance (by the bride). It will include varying configurations of people, such as the following:

- The bride with all her bridesmaids
- The bride with each bridesmaid individually
- The bride, the groom, and her bridesmaids
- The bride, the groom, her bridesmaids, and his groomsmen
- The bridesmaids and groomsmen alone

Of course, for the bride, this list will be much longer, to include various configurations of family members from each side of the family. Often, the bride and groom will complete their list of formal shots with the bridal party and then set you free to celebrate as they pose for portraits on their own.

Bridesmaids on Film

Do you dread the thought of formal portraits because you feel you're simply not photogenic? Anyone can improve their percentages (of good photos to bad) by heeding the following tips.

 Fact

If you are lucky, the bride will have made arrangements to have some refreshments and hors d'oeuvres brought to the wedding party where the photo session is taking place—a little pick me up before the reception!

Get a Good Night's Sleep

Nothing ruins your look more certainly than tired-looking eyes or a saggy, bloated face caused by lack of sleep, or worse, a hangover. Unlike men, women can at least allay some of the damage with makeup. Still, it's amazing how the camera picks up imperfections you won't even notice in the mirror.

Look Your Best

Having your hair professionally styled and your makeup professionally applied can go a long way toward taking great pictures. This is particularly true if you don't regularly wear makeup. A too-pale face can cause you to look washed out in photos.

Touch Up Immediately Before You Take Pictures

Take care of those stray hairs coming loose or that spinach stuck in your teeth. Reapply lipstick, and make sure your bra strap isn't showing. A last-minute look in the mirror is insurance against photo mishaps. Carry a small compact, some pressed powder, lipstick, and lip gloss in your wedding-day bag to ensure you look fresh for photos all day long.

🄴❗ Alert

Be sure to have the bride pack a little bag for touch ups, and be sure to have it easily accessible for after the ceremony. Of course you want to look great, but it is her big day!

Show Off Your Best Angle

If you are not sure of your best angle, examine other pictures you've liked of yourself. Look at which side of your face is pictured; what position your body is in, where your arms and hands fall, and how your hair is styled. For example, you'll always look trimmer if you turn your body at a slight angle toward the camera, rather than letting yourself be photographed straight on. In addition, your face probably has a more flattering side for photographs, and even the angle at which you hold your head can make a big difference.

Stand or Sit Up Straight

Slouching and poor posture will definitely show up in photos. Straighten your back and lift your shoulders for the most flattering pose.

Smile

A smile is the best accessory! There's nothing like a big smile to make you look great on film. Think of something that makes you happy—your new boyfriend, your dog, or your Hello Kitty collection—to elicit a big natural smile right before the photographer snaps.

Show Time

There is a lot going on behind the scenes on the wedding day. There is set up, getting dressed, traveling to and from locations, and photography. So what should you expect at the ceremony? What, specifically, will your role be and how can you best fulfill it? Some of these answers will depend on whether or not the bride has a wedding planner, or how involved her mother is, or how much of a control freak she is.

💫 Essential

Although your role may be largely ceremonial by this stage of the game, be prepared. The bride or her family or another bridesmaid could call on you at any minute for some last-minute assistance.

Ceremonial Role

Ironically, most of the bridesmaids' work is done by the time the ceremony takes place. All the shower planning, bachelorette-party planning, bride hand-holding, errand-running, and moral supporting will be history by the time you reach that ceremony site, at which point your duties are largely ceremonial. If you're the maid of honor, you have some specific, tangible tasks to perform, such as signing the marriage license and participating in the ring ceremony; but as a regular bridesmaid, you'll really just have to smile, look pretty, and have fun.

We're Here . . . Now What?

Though you've rehearsed it the night before, the ceremony will still hold some surprises, particularly how long it may feel. That's because you've probably only rehearsed the recessional and processional, not the entire ceremony. The average wedding ceremony lasts only an hour—a reasonable amount of time, surely. It's also an hour during which you'll still find yourself front and center, where good behavior is a must.

 Alert

Avoid bringing extra attention to yourself during the ceremony—stifle that laugh, refrain from fidgeting or looking around, and certainly do not talk! You are on stage, so be on your best behavior.

At some ceremonies, the bridesmaids will be provided a row of seats in which to relax during the majority of the ceremony; at other ceremonies, you'll be expected to stand throughout. While an hour of standing may not seem like a lot, it can become pretty tiring, especially if you're balancing on new high heels in front of a hundred or more people.

The Longest Aisle

Your first obvious public role as bridesmaid will be your walk down the aisle. At the rehearsal, you will learn the order of your descent, which is often based on height—shortest bridesmaids followed by taller ones. The last wedding attendant to walk down the aisle is the maid of honor. If there is a flower girl, she will immediately precede the bride, throwing rose petals in her path. As you walk down the aisle, all eyes will fall on you. This can certainly be disconcerting, especially if the spotlight is not something you enjoy. However, it will be over before you know it.

Grace Under Pressure

As with any major event or moment, if you think you look your best, you'll feel more comfortable when your walk down the aisle makes you the center of attention. That means ensuring your dress fits properly (not too tight or too loose, or you'll fidget with it), your hair and makeup are looking good, and you're wearing the right undergarments. The following tips will help you make the walk with grace under pressure.

ⓔ✱ Essential

Be sure you've thought about what you'll be wearing under your dress before the big day. Wear (or purchase) a bra that will provide enough support and won't show under your dress. And be sure to choose hosiery in the correct size.

Smile

If you feel weird smiling at nothing in particular, don't worry—it will look a lot weirder if you're stone faced or frowning. For added inspiration to flash those pearly whites, make eye contact with a friendly face in the congregation. Give him or her a smile, and make it last.

Stand Up Straight

As your mother always admonished, don't slouch. Walk tall and you'll exude confidence.

Break in the Shoes

If you're wearing new shoes, break them in before the wedding day so they're more comfortable on your feet and there's some wear on the soles. There are few greater wedding-day hazards than slippery new shoes on a smooth aisle runner or carpeting. Wear them around the house so they'll be comfortable and safe for walking on the wedding day.

 Fact

> The most common bridesmaid offense is walking down the aisle at warp speed. Take your time and walk elegantly, at a slow pace. Even if it feels too slow, it's probably not.

Keep Your Eyes Looking Forward and Your Head Steady

An occasional glance to your right and your left is fine, but move your head and eyes too much and you'll risk some strange expressions in the ensuing photo proofs. Not that it's all about the pictures, of course.

During the Ceremony

Unless you are the maid of honor, which means you'll be assisting the bride with straightening her train, holding her bouquet, or participating in the ring ceremony, you'll have little to do besides stand (or sit) and watch as the ceremony unfolds. Depending on the ceremony's religious rituals or traditions, the bride and groom may greet you individually during a sign of peace interlude, or you may be offered communion (if you so desire). However, aside from these specific rituals, there's little to do besides be an observant guest, like those seated behind you.

After the Ceremony

Of course, you'll spring right back into action after the groom kisses his bride, smashes the glass, or helps the bride jump the broom, whatever cultural or religious ritual signifies the end of their particular ceremony. You will have reviewed at the rehearsal what to do during the recessional (you walk back down the aisle). Most likely, at the head of the aisle, you will meet your partner groomsman, who will offer his arm to escort you to the back of the ceremony site.

 **Essential**

When you walk the aisle, hold your bouquet correctly. Relax your arms, so that your elbows bend slightly at the waist. The bouquet should be held at approximately waist height, and tilted slightly forward so that the top of the bouquet is visible as you walk.

The wedding party will immediately follow the bride and groom, and no doubt there will be much music and photo flashing as you make your way to the back of the ceremony site. For this walk, you can be much more relaxed and natural. You may greet guests if you wish as you pass them on your way out.

Once you've reached the back of the church or synagogue (or wherever the ceremony's taken place), the bride may ask that you participate in a receiving line. The receiving line is just what it sounds like: a lineup of the bride, groom, their parents, and the wedding party who greet guests as they exit the ceremony. In some cases, the bride may wish to keep her receiving line moving more quickly and efficiently, in which case the bridesmaids and groomsmen won't be included in the receiving line (though the maid of honor and best man will probably still participate).

e✔ Fact

As an alternate plan, the receiving line may also be formed to greet guests as they enter the reception. This is usually the case if there is a time delay between the ceremony and reception or if the ceremony and reception are at different locations.

If there is a receiving line and you're not included, you'll have a few minutes to relax and unwind before the next phase of the wedding. If you're feeling productive, you may wish to help organize the bride and groom's traditional exit from the ceremony site, by passing out the "rice" (usually birdseed now, as raw rice can injure birds trying to ingest it), bubbles, or flower petals (or anything else the guests will be tossing in celebration).

Immediately before the bride and groom exit the site, help line up guests on either side of the door to greet the bride and groom as they emerge as husband and wife for the first time. Their exit is usually followed by more mingling outside the ceremony site (unless it's raining or snowing). If you're on a tight time schedule, as you will be if you have loads of pictures to take before you get to the reception, you can help organize your group's exit. Gracefully usher the bride and groom away from enthusiastic guests and toward the photo site or the limousine that will take them there.

The Reception and Beyond

You made it down the aisle, smiled pretty, fluffed a train, held a bouquet, and now it's finally time to relax and really celebrate, right? Not quite. The most popular type of wedding reception begins in the early evening with a cocktail hour, followed by a meal, followed by dancing. Interspersed are a number of time-honored traditions that you, as bridesmaid, may also be a part of.

Your Best Behavior

By virtue of your telltale dress, you'll still stand out among the other wedding guests, so try to behave as the bride's goodwill emissary even after your duties have officially ended. You'll continue to attract attention as the evening progresses, so save the dirty dancing, heavy drinking, and chain smoking for another evening (or at least for the after-hours party). You don't want to create any mini-scandals at this family event, and you don't want to be forever known for inappropriate behavior among people who've never even met you. Drinking too much alcohol, playing bridesmaid diva, or sneaking off with a cute groomsman may sound fun to you, but it will not make a good impression with the bride, groom, or their families.

Traditions and Duties

Aside from being on your best behavior, what are your more tangible duties as the reception unfolds? Obviously, every wedding is different. Not every bride will include every tradition in her wedding, and some brides will add new ones. This section covers some of the more common wedding-day traditions that you can expect to include you.

 Fact

> Even though the ceremony's over, your bridesmaid duties may not be. Be prepared to take part in reception traditions that may include the bouquet toss, the wedding party dance, and more.

The Formal Introduction

There is a practice at some weddings that immediately follows cocktail hour and immediately precedes the serving of the meal, when everyone is seated. This is the formal announcement of the bridal party and the bride and groom to the rest of the wedding guests. Typically, the DJ or band emcee will announce each member of the bridal party, including groomsmen, bridesmaids, the best man, and the maid of honor. When your name is announced, you will enter the reception room and walk to your seat.

Bridal Party Seating

If the wedding calls for a traditional seating plan, expect to sit at a long head table with seating on one side only. Seated at the table will be the bride and groom, the maid of honor and best man, and the bridesmaids and groomsmen. Often, this table is raised on a platform so guests can better view the wedding party. Traditionally, seating is boy/girl with the bride and groom at the center, the maid of honor next to the groom, the best man next to the bride, and so on until everyone is seated.

Typically, children in the bridal party are seated elsewhere, with their parents.

However, this traditional seating plan has loosened in recent years. While many weddings still adhere to it, other couples are choosing to adopt alternative seating arrangements. Some brides find that designating traditional guest tables in favorable positions for the wedding party provide a more social atmosphere, as is seating the wedding party with their dates or spouses (instead of across the room from them, which often happens when the traditional head table is used). This is wholly dependent on the preferences of the bride and groom, and you probably won't know your seating arrangement until you actually arrive at the reception and pick up your place card.

Fact

The traditional head table is the table at which the bride, groom, and bridal party are seated for dinner. It is usually a long, rectangular table at which you'll be seated only on one side, facing outward toward the wedding guests.

Some weddings don't have formal seating at all. This type of wedding is designed to promote mingling and dancing over sitting at one table for a long length of time. There are no place cards, so you'll largely be on your own.

Bridal Party Dance

Another tradition that seems to be losing some of its old-time popularity is the bridal party dance. This dance among the wedding party typically follows the bride's dance with her father. If the bride chooses to incorporate this tradition, you'll be expected to dance to one song with your groomsman partner while all the guests look on.

🅔❓ Question

How do I know whom I am supposed to dance with during the bridal party dance?
The groomsman you dance with is typically the one who escorted you up the aisle following the wedding ceremony. Perhaps he's someone you've been waiting to dance with all night . . . but if he's not, be polite and courteous. This is tradition, after all—you don't have to go home with the guy.

Bridal Party Toasts

Traditionally, the best man and the father of the bride offer wedding day toasts, and the father of the groom sometimes joins them. But in recent years this tradition, too, has loosened, and more and more honored guests are offering up a few words, particularly the maid of honor. If the floor seems open to multiple toasts, you, too, may wish to take the opportunity to say a few words. If you'd prefer a smaller, more intimate crowd, you may also consider offering your toast/speech at the rehearsal dinner. If you do plan to add a few words at the wedding reception, be sure to let the bride or groom know in advance, so that they can alert the emcee or DJ to pass the mike to you at the appropriate time.

The Bouquet Toss

No wedding event is more universally symbolized in movies, soap operas, or chick lit than the (oft-dreaded) bouquet toss. This tradition, once a benign practice meant to symbolize the bride's goodwill toward the bridesmaids, is now often viewed with dread. But why does a seemingly innocent tradition, in which the bride tosses her bouquet to the unattached female guests, cause so much controversy?

 Fact

The best toasts are short and to the point. You may want to tell a funny anecdote, a sentimental story, or just offer your best wishes on behalf of the bridesmaids.

First, the tradition's very nature separates female guests into those who are engaged or married from those who are single, and this is often a touchy subject. Many unattached women may not wish to be "singled" out publicly, especially if they're sensitive about their marital status. Some women simply feel this practice is loaded with negative symbolism, by placing her entire gender in a clamoring position to be the next one married. Of course, some women simply view the bouquet toss as a harmless, fun tradition that shouldn't be taken so seriously. Especially those under the age of fifteen, who think it's great fun.

Garter Toss

The bouquet-toss tradition is also sometimes extended to include the men, with a brother tradition called the garter toss. First, the groom makes a lighthearted show of removing the bride's garter from beneath her wedding dress. Then, the groom tosses the garter over his shoulder, to be caught by one of the single male guests who've assembled behind him. Then, the lucky grabber of the garter places the garter onto the leg of the woman who's caught the bouquet while the guests look on.

Obviously, not every woman will enjoy a stranger moving up, up, up her thigh with a garter in a public forum, which is probably another reason women have begun avoiding the bouquet toss in recent years. Again, if you find yourself in this situation, try to make light of it and enjoy the attention. Give the garter guy a hard time, and make a funny show of it. Guests will appreciate the sense of humor on that cute, sassy bridesmaid who caught the bouquet.

e✔ Fact

As one of the most recognizable female guests at the wedding, you are expected to be at the center of this tradition (unless you're married, that is). If the bride chooses to include the bouquet toss, be enthusiastic and lighthearted about it.

After Hours

Of course, the party isn't over 'til it's over. After most weddings, you'll usually find a group of stragglers willing to forge ahead, celebrating even more. If the bride and groom are among them, more power to them—they don't want this party to end, and why should they, really? After all, you only get married once. Well, half the people do, anyway. Whether the newlyweds are in attendance or not, heed the following tips when signing on for after hours.

Go Home or Close to Home

Invite guests back to your house or the hotel bar (or hotel room, if it's large enough). Don't start barhopping unless you have prearranged transportation, like cabs or a limo.

Prearrange for Some Drinks and Snacks

Buy a few bottles of wine or champagne in advance, and have some bottled water, coffee, and snacks available for those who wish to sober up.

Don't Harass the Bride and Groom

This is often a favorite pastime of wedding guests under the influence, and in fact is a reason why many newlyweds keep their hotel whereabouts a secret. Even if it's all in good fun, the bride and groom have better things to do than endure your attention, even if it's just catching up on some sleep before their honeymoon.

 Fact

There is historical significance to the garter toss, which stems back a couple hundred years. Superstition held that a woman presented with another bride's garter would remain faithful to the man who gave it to her.

Be Mentally Prepared for the Next Day

After many weddings, you'll be invited to attend a postwedding brunch or a party at someone's home as a final sendoff before the wedding weekend is over. Exhaustion or a hangover won't make you enjoy it any more. In fact, either factor could make a brunch (and potential travel home afterward) akin to torture. Try to get to bed relatively early, and drink lots of water before dozing off.

CHAPTER 10

Every Wedding Is Unique

Even under the most ideal conditions—huge budgets, cooperative families—this is real life, and with that is the potential that something will go awry. Under most circumstances, your responsibilities as bridesmaid will remain the same, but there are some situations that may prompt you to do things a little differently. There is a full range of unexpected or unusual circumstances that may arise during the wedding you're participating in. Keep reading . . . and be prepared!

Second Weddings

There's nothing unusual about a second wedding. In fact, four out of ten weddings in the United States are the second wedding for one or both partners. The only unusual aspect about them is that they may incorporate philosophies or practices that could alter your role as a traditional bridesmaid, though even that is not a foregone conclusion. In recent years, second weddings have become more and more like first weddings, rather than the quieter, more intimate events of the past.

 Fact

Second weddings account for approximately 44 percent of all U.S. weddings. While they're not uncommon, there are some special considerations for you as bridesmaid—such as whether to throw a shower and a bachelorette party.

What's Different?

Just like every first wedding is different, so is every second wedding. There's no way to lump them into one category, or to predict what tone any individual party will take. Ultimately, it will be up to the bride and groom to determine what style wedding they have. Some brides may choose to pull out all the stops, including the big white dress, the big white cake, and the huge guest list, especially if they didn't have it the first time around.

Other brides may feel that a large, elaborate wedding is inappropriate, impractical, or too similar to their first weddings. In this case, they may wish to have a less formal tone, fewer guests, or a simpler ceremony. If the bride plans on holding a scaled-down affair, your wedding-day duties may be significantly fewer, too, with a loosening of certain traditions. As with any wedding, follow the bride's lead for guidance.

Parties and More Parties

So, that's that, but what about those prewedding responsibilities, like planning the shower and bachelorette party? Are these parties even appropriate for a second wedding, and if so, are the bridesmaids still responsible for hosting them? The answer to these questions depends on the individual bride.

e★ Essential

You should treat this wedding just as you would a bride's first wedding. It's no less special or meaningful an occasion, and if you've agreed to be a bridesmaid, you've agreed to all the formalities that go with it.

Showers

From an etiquette perspective, a shower is a perfectly appropriate occasion for a second wedding. As such, the maid of honor and bridesmaids have a duty to plan one, if the bride so desires. There may be brides, however, who wish not to have a shower. Perhaps she's uncomfortable about being on the receiving end of gifts again, for instance, especially if her first wedding wasn't far in the past. If this is the case but you'd still like to honor the bride by bringing her close family and friends together before the wedding, you can still plan a no-gifts party or specify a charity for donations in lieu of gifts.

Bachelorette Parties

When it comes to bachelorette parties, (as has been said before) the bride should make her wishes known on the topic.

Some second-time brides may feel one bachelorette party in a lifetime is plenty, while others may crave all the fun and excitement that surround a wedding. This will largely depend on the bride's specific circumstances and her personality.

ⓔ! Alert

Before you begin planning a shower or bachelorette party for a bride's second wedding, determine her comfort level. There's a possibility she may not want a lot of hoopla for either event.

Gender Bender

While this topic has been covered, there is a little more to the situation and it should be addressed. There has been a continually increasing trend to have a bridesman or groomswoman. Many marrying couples have close relationships that cross gender barriers, and they wouldn't dream of excluding close friends or family members from participating in the wedding simply because they're not the same sex.

What to Wear?

Certainly, this trend does not mean that men have to don a bridesmaid dress and women have to rent a tux (though the woman-in-tux thing is a little easier to digest). Usually, a woman who's close with the groom will wear the same outfit as the bridesmaids, and a man serving for the bride will wear whatever the groomsmen are wearing.

How Will It Work?

This gender bending can lead to questions. For instance, just because you'll be dressed as a bridesmaid (but are technically a groomsman), does it mean you have to act as one, with all the traditional shower-planning and bachelorette-hosting duties that go with it? Will you be invited to the bachelor party? How, exactly, will this whole thing work?

e🄯 Alert

If you're serving as bridesmaid for the groom, keep the lines of communication open. When in doubt about your duties, ask. The bride will probably be the one with the most opinions here.

Very likely, if the bride and groom have included you, they've thought out all the contingencies. Which means that, with any luck, you can simply refer to them with any uncertainties. Perhaps they'll decide against having gender-specific parties, preferring a coed shower and mixed bachelor/bachelorette party, especially if they both have a mixed social circle. Or maybe they have no interest in these traditional conventions anyway, in which case you won't have to worry at all.

There is a chance, however, that you'll be lumped in with the rest of the bridesmaids. You probably would have been invited to these events anyway, as a close friend of the groom's. If you have developed a relationship with the bride, you can surely expect an invitation. If you've never met her (and by extension, her bridesmaids), your participation might feel a bit more awkward.

What Should I Do?

If you are unsure of your role and it has not been made clear to you by the bride or groom, your best bet is always to err on the side of caution. It never hurts to offer assistance, and you'll figure out soon enough if your help is wanted or not. When all else fails, simply communicate your questions or uncertainty to the groom. He, too, should offer guidance regarding how he'd like the situation to work, especially when it comes to attending that bachelor party.

🄮❓ Question

As a groomswoman, will I be expected to help host the bridal shower?
There's no formal etiquette that dictates what to do in this scenario. If the maid of honor is contacting you with the details, you'll probably be expected to participate. If she hasn't contacted you, it probably means she's treating you as if you were a traditional groomsman. Just ask!

The Wedding That Never Happened

Yes, unfortunately, it happens—weddings get canceled. While you may or may not know the reasons yet, there's one thing you definitely don't know, and that's what to do next. There are hurt feelings involved, money spent and lost, and a whole lot of questions left answered.

What's the Situation?

Needless to say, this is a difficult and complex situation. No doubt the bride (and groom) is completely devastated, even if it was she who ultimately called it off. There may have been dramatic circumstances initiating their breakup; perhaps it was long in coming; or maybe they didn't break up at all, but simply postponed the wedding until an undetermined date. No matter what the circumstances, this couple's problems will be subject to the public eye due to the widely announced impending nuptials.

Show of Support

Before you consider your own circumstances as a canceled bridesmaid, try to consider your friend, the bride. Not only is the relationship with the man she loves suffering (or over), but it's also happened in a very public forum. In addition to her sadness about the relationship, she's probably also feeling guilty and embarrassed about canceling the wedding.

 **Essential**

> If the wedding is canceled, your most important duty as bridesmaid is to lend an ear or a shoulder to cry on. The bride will undoubtedly need a great deal of moral support, whether it was her decision to cancel or not.

Try to be a supportive, helpful friend. Don't call her the next day to find out what you should do with your bridesmaid dress; don't ask her whether the store will take back your shoes; and don't inquire about returning the shower gift you gave her. In other words, don't make her feel worse than she already does. There will be plenty of time once things have calmed down to take care of practical matters. Your job now, as a bridesmaid (and a friend), is to offer a shoulder to cry on and plenty of moral support.

The Practical Matters

Beyond the emotional issues, there are practical ones. If you can't bother the bride about them, what should you do? Again, that depends on the circumstances. If the wedding's simply been postponed and not canceled, hang on to your dress and all the accoutrements until further notice. If it has been officially canceled, keep the dress for a suitable period of time—a month or two—then decide what to do with it.

 Fact

> If the wedding has been canceled very close to the wedding date, you may wish to offer your help to the bride's family, writing notes or making phone calls to inform invited guests about the cancellation.

You can try to contact the shop where the dress was purchased, but with few exceptions, most bridal shops will not accept returns on wedding or bridesmaid dresses. One option is to keep it, if you think you'll wear it to some other occasion. You can also sell it through a consignment shop, classified ad, or online at an auction site like eBay. Of course, if you think there's any chance the wedding will be rescheduled as originally planned, don't sell the dress, or you may have to buy another one at full price again.

If you've already sent a wedding gift, you should expect to receive it back. In addition, etiquette dictates that the bride should return all engagement and shower gifts to the gift giver, provided they have not been used. Again, if the bride is slow to take care of these practical issues, cut her some slack or offer your help to package and send items back to the gift givers, if you think she'd welcome it.

Keeping Perspective

It is natural to feel resentful that you've spent so much time, effort, and money on an event that never happened, but keep things in perspective. While you may be out a few bucks, the bride is out a fiancé, not to mention her entire idea of the future. Surely, it was never her intention to dupe you or the many other loving friends and family with whom she celebrated her engagement.

🔴 Alert

Neither the bride nor you are obligated to explain to anyone why the wedding was canceled. Use your discretion, and look to the bride to determine how much information to give. She may prefer that most of the details remain private.

Personally Speaking

Just because you're a bridesmaid doesn't mean the rest of your life stops, even if you suspect the bride sometimes wishes it would. It does mean that sometimes your own life can get in the way of being the best bridesmaid you can be. Unfortunately, we can't always control when big or stressful life events occur. Some factors that arise may be perfectly legitimate excuses for shirking your bridesmaid duties; others are probably just that—excuses.

Common Dilemmas

When and if the times comes that wedding plans are interrupted by life, consult the following list to determine the potential results of various life complications and how they reflect on and affect you as a bridesmaid.

Dilemma: You break up with your boyfriend in the months leading up to the wedding.

Poison potential: Being a bridesmaid only exaggerates your own loneliness. In fact, you've begun despising all things couple-related. You find yourself blowing off bridesmaid duties, and your cynicism is beginning to affect (and annoy) all the other bridesmaids. Plus, you dread attending the wedding dateless.

How to deal: Make being the world's best bridesmaid your personal pet project. Take all that energy you formerly spent on your boyfriend and invest it in the bride. It will not only distract you from your woes, it will help the bride and bring you closer. At the wedding (to distract you from your solo status), keep busy with bridesmaids' tasks. Possibly even scope out the grooms-men and single male guests, if you are ready for that.

Dilemma: You lose your job during the engagement.

Poison potential: Your self-esteem takes a major dip, not to mention your bank account. You're worried enough about paying your gas bill without worrying about buying that pair of overpriced shoes. You begin avoiding the bride and the other bridesmaids, hoping this commitment will somehow just go away.

How to deal: Talk to the bride. Tell her your circumstances. If she's a true friend, she'll either help you foot the bill or let you off the hook with no hard feelings. She might also let you par-ticipate on a smaller scale, like giving you a reading or other honored task to perform.

Dilemma: You move away.

Poison potential: You can barely keep track of where you packed your kitchenware, much less the details of this wedding. Between moving away from town and reorganizing your life, you've definitely been lax in your bridesmaid duties.

How to deal: Pick up the pace. While this is surely a stressful time for you, you did commit to being a bridesmaid, so do all you can to honor that commitment. Try to participate as much as you can, despite the distance. Keep in touch with the bride and bridesmaids via phone calls or e-mails. Try to attend prewedding events when possible.

Dilemma: You and the bride have a falling out.

Poison potential: Perhaps she's become Bridezilla and you've had as much as you can stand, or perhaps she's confronted you with some perceived transgression. No matter what the circumstances, bridal resentment is certainly not inspiring you to be an enthusiastic bridesmaid.

How to deal: A conflict with the bride during this emotionally charged time could be devastating to a friendship. Tread carefully. Try to face the conflict openly and get past it by having a heart-to-heart with the bride. You definitely want to mend fences before the wedding, and ignoring the problem or avoiding the bride won't help matters.

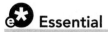 **Essential**

If you think the bride is acting unreasonably, try to extend your patience. The stress of the wedding may be causing her to act in ways she normally wouldn't. Presumably, she'll be back to normal posthoneymoon.

Dilemma: Family obligations become overwhelming.

Poison potential: You've helped the bride with many prewedding tasks, but suddenly you've got some family obligations that demand more of your time—a grandparent who's ill, a child who needs attention, marital difficulties—and while you'd like to help more, there simply aren't enough hours in the day.

How to deal: Explain your situation to the bride, and if she is a true friend, she'll be more than understanding. If you feel comfortable doing so, you may also wish to alert the bridesmaids about your circumstances, in case you need their help with wedding-related duties.

Dilemma: You become ill before the big day.

Poison potential: Obviously, your health takes precedence over everything else in your life. However, if you've fallen ill, you may be feeling guilty for not participating enough or for knowing you won't be able to carry out your bridesmaid duties.

How to deal: If you've been struck with a temporary illness right before the wedding, such as the stomach flu, let the bride know as soon as possible. Then try to do as much as you can, such as participating in the ceremony but skipping the reception. Obviously, there may be cases when you're simply too weak to do anything. If it's a more serious, chronic condition, you should also alert the bride. She will understand if it prevents you from performing your full range of duties.

Dilemma: There's a death in your family.

Poison potential: This is a worst-case, emergency scenario.

How to deal: In the event that someone close to you becomes ill or dies immediately preceding the wedding date, you'll need to use your best judgment. Obviously, if services conflict with the wedding, you will have to skip the wedding. If you are grieving, you may also feel as if you're not up for a happy event, but keep in mind that participating may also serve as therapy. Being surrounded by close friends and/or family can alleviate your feelings of isolation. In any case, do what feels right to you.

Dilemma: There's a death in the bride's or groom's family.

Poison potential: Another worst-case scenario.

How to deal: In the unfortunate event of a death in the bride's or groom's family close to the wedding date, there's a chance the event may be canceled. If so, you may wish to offer your help to the family by calling to inform wedding guests. The bride and groom may also decide that it's best if the event went on as planned or with certain modifications. Follow the bride's lead when it comes to changes to the original plans.

Postwedded Bliss

The wedding is over . . . so is the drama, right? Wrong! Unusual or unexpected circumstances can also occur after the wedding date. In fact, dealing with your friend as a newly married person is an unusual circumstance unto itself. Even if everything leading up to the wedding has gone just fine—you helped plan a great shower and an eventful bachelorette party, and you even managed to walk down the aisle with no major stumbles— there's another world to deal with beyond the wedding day.

 **Essential**

For some brides, life won't change at all after she starts going by Mrs.; for others, everything changes. Be aware of how this may affect your friendship.

It's All Changed

The first year of marriage for a couple, especially two relatively young people who've never gone through it before, can be extremely stressful and difficult. This is partly because no one's bothered to think about life beyond the wedding day. Many brides are so consumed with wedding and honeymoon planning that they haven't stopped to think about the major changes in store, like the following:

- Leaving the security of home
- Suddenly sharing everything with her man, from the bathroom to the phone to finances
- Sleeping with someone else in her bed—every night
- Checking with her husband on major purchases and other big decisions
- Running a household
- Giving up her single-girl spontaneity and independence

Taken all at once, these changes can be a bit overwhelming, even if they are what the bride has dreamed about her whole young life. Plus, many brides experience postwedding depression, due to the inevitable drop in activity, excitement, and attention once the engagement and honeymoon are over.

🄴✔ Fact

Make a genuine effort to get along with the bride's new husband. The better friends you become, the more you'll see your friend—with or without him around.

Being Friends with a Mrs.

What does this marriage of hers mean to you, her brides-maid and friend? How will her marriage affect you and your friendship? It would be easy to say nothing will change, but it's more likely that her marriage will affect some aspects of your friendship, for better or worse. Your fun-loving single gal pal is now a Mrs. With a new ring came new responsibilities and loy-alties. While the friendship will change, it does not have to be for the worse. You both just have to get used to the new relation-ship you have with the Mrs.

With a new husband comes a new routine. While she shouldn't give up on her outside interests entirely, she may need to compromise some of her old routines in the name of spend-ing time with her husband, at least in the short term. Give her some time. If she's not back by the next television sweeps sea-son, start laying on the guilt.

Essential

The first year of marriage can be very difficult on the bride, as she settles into a new life and a new routine. This may mean your friendship will experience changes as well. Be prepared and patient and you'll both weather any storms.

Flexibility

Those last-minute shopping trips to Manhattan may be a little more difficult to pull off now. As are the weekends in the Caribbean and cross-state road trips; even that day trip to the beach has become a struggle to plan. The fact is that your friend and her new hubby will probably be making a wholehearted newlywed effort to coordinate all their time off together, which means excursions with you won't be her top priority. Does this mean you've lost a travel partner? That you'll need to start jock-eying for a new best friend?

Even if those weeklong road trips are a thing of the past, you can still try to corral her company for a weekend with the girls, or even an overnighter. The key is compromise. Try to under-stand that she's in the throes of newlywed bliss right now, and that this, too, shall pass. Be patient while she figures out how to divvy up her free time with all the people now in her life, includ-ing her husband, family, in-laws, and friends.

Intimacy

You used to share every minute detail of your lives, from your latest blind dates to your sexual experiences, now you feel she's holding back. What's up with that?

 Alert

> Once she's married, your friendship with the bride will probably change in some ways, at least temporarily, as she adjusts to a completely new lifestyle. Try to roll with the changes and offer extra amounts of patience, and your relationship will continue to grow and evolve.

Many women feel they're betraying their husbands if they reveal the negative aspects of their marriages, like disagree-ments, disappointments, or other conflicts. Especially during the first year of marriage, many new brides feel as if admitting to problems means they have problem marriages, when in fact they're simply having completely normal growing pains.

It's also normal if some of the allegiance she shared with you shifts to her husband, who has, after all, become her number-one life partner (even if you are her best friend). As difficult as it may be to deal with, her husband may become her primary confidant, a role you're used to filling. That might hurt, but try to understand. You can still be just as close, even if sharing her is sometimes a drag. Finally, try not to resent her new husband, or the problem may only become worse.

As far as the sex talk goes, once someone is married (or in a serious relationship), what happens in the bedroom should generally stay in the bedroom, which means the details you used to share so openly with your friend may be a done deal. After all, would you want your future husband sharing his intimate experiences with you with his buddies in the locker room? These experiences should be sacred between husband and wife, and as such, you should respect her privacy, even if you're used to getting all the details.

🅔❗ Alert

It will do nothing but hurt your friendship with the bride if the groom dislikes you. Unfortunately, many female friendships have been known to suffer because a newlywed's spouse doesn't get along with her friends.

Patience

She never minded those 2 A.M. postdate phone calls before. Now she's screening her calls or blowing you off until the next day. You need a Sunday morning quarterback/date analyst now, not after your buzz has worn off. What's a girl to do? Remember, your late-night phone call affects not just your friend but also her new roommate: her husband. Save it for the morning. There are new boundaries you have to learn, and this is one of them.

Lifestyle

Maybe you used to head out to the clubs most weekends for a few cocktails and dancing, or maybe you could count on her to join you for a fairly regular happy hour or weeknight dinner. It's possible that now that she's settled she may forgo some of your old routines; in fact, she may have already begun doing so during the engagement period. Many women feel that once they've met the man of their dreams, they can give up the single life in favor of the Blockbuster night.

Again, this may be temporary. Give her some time to cocoon with her husband, and be there when she emerges; chances are it's a temporary state . . . though temporary can sometimes mean a year or two. Rest assured that once she's settled into her role as wife, marital bliss will inevitably demand a taste of the old single life from time to time.

CHAPTER 11

It Could Happen to You

You may have heard the saying, "Truth is stranger than fiction." That seems to ring especially true with weddings. Maybe it's the emotion, maybe it's the money, maybe it's the extraordinary expectations, but weddings seem to bring on more than their fair share of conflicts, imagined tragedies, emotional meltdowns, and mini-disasters. No matter what you have heard, no matter what you believe, just remember, it could happen to you.

Bridesmaid Foibles

As a bridesmaid, there is the chance you will find yourself in a situation that could range from unconventional to uncomfortable to out of control. It may be the bride, it may be the groom, it may be her family; in fact, it may even be you! And of course, there is the chance it is simply circumstances. You better believe real-life circumstances are better than anything ever made up for the movies.

Essential

Being a bridesmaid can be fun and it can be stressful. Common sense and understanding are the keys to making the day and this experience all that you imagine it can be.

A Little Tipsy

Unfortunately, nerves, stress, emotions, and numerous other factors may cause what's normally an acceptable number of libations to affect a girl in the strangest of ways. Alcohol can be the catalyst to many a major situation. Be aware of how one too many drinks can sneak up on anyone and cause a ruckus.

Too Young and Too Much

Often, at these big celebrations, not-quite-of-age bridesmaids will attempt to take advantage of the situation and partake in some adult libations. Many an underage bridesmaid has tried to convince a bartender she was more than old enough to indulge. Taking into account age and the possibility of exploiting the situation by ordering a large number of drinks, a bridesmaid can find herself "done in" before the night really begins.

A good example is this tale of one bride's underage twin sisters, who were able to pull one over on the bartender, along with some assistance from some older groomsmen. By dinner they could barely stand. Fortunately, the wedding was taking place in a hotel ballroom, so the bride's father was able to escort them to their room, and after some coffee, water, and a few admonishing words, they promptly passed out. The next day, they not only had to deal with some nasty hangovers, but they also became the punch line for out-of-town family and friends who gathered at the bride's family's home for a postnuptial celebratory brunch.

Fact

Most wedding venues have safety and legal precautions in place to avoid underage drinking. They need to make sure the guests are safe and that they obey the law. Liability laws vary from state to state, but underage drinking is serious business.

The Seasoned Partygoer

On the other hand, you may find a seasoned partygoer drinking a little too much during the preparty festivities and continuing on this cycle, not even realizing it, over the course of the day. With a long lag between the ceremony and the reception, there is much opportunity to partake in some partying. One too many bottles of "happiness" during the ride to the reception or during the photo shoot can put a bridesmaid out for the night, or for a good portion of it.

A Little Too Hot

During those summer weddings, high temperatures are a dangerous mix with alcohol. When the temperature is into the

90s or above, don't count on the air conditioning to save you. It is easy to keep drinking without realizing how the heat and the drinks are mixing, or more likely not mixing. A few too many cocktails, not nearly enough dinner, and high heat can leave you feeling dizzy and a bit sick.

 Alert

> Be careful about drinking alcohol on the day of the wedding. The nervousness and excitement of the day can cause you to drink more than you intended to, potentially ruining your day. It is a celebration, but you need to pace yourself, or choose to abstain.

Forgettable Fashion

When your friend gets engaged, there is always a rush of excitement. And there is always one friend who is the master of the party—everything she does is picture perfect. No doubt, this will extend into her wedding planning, and she expects a certain level of commitment from the bridesmaids, too. So what to do when you miss a beat or forget an integral part of your carefully selected ensemble?

 Alert

> Be sure your bridesmaid dress and all accessories are pressed and ready to go the day before the wedding. You'll avoid stress and headaches from last-minute emergencies.

Most situations have a solution, but how they play out is quite different. Take the case of these two bridesmaids who flew in for their friend's wedding, only to realize once they got there that they had their strapless dresses, but had left their matching shawls at home. Not only was the shawl a very important component of the wedding look, it was also necessary, as no bare shoulders were allowed during the ceremony.

So what happens next? If you are lucky and there is enough time, have someone overnight the shawl (or missing accessory) to you. If that is not an option, call local dress shops and bridal salons to see if they carry the item or something similar. If all else fails, a trip to the local fabric store may be in order. There is the possibility that a seamstress or tailor may be able to help. For a shawl, it is quite easy to fake it, but for some other items it may not be as easy.

Essential

If you are the maid of honor or the take-charge type, make a list of must brings and e-mail it to the bridesmaids (with the bride's blessing, of course). Checklists are good and can save everyone a lot of last-minute headaches.

A better solution is to try to avoid this conundrum altogether. Make a checklist and check it twice . . . maybe even three times, especially if you are traveling. Talk to the other bridesmaids about what they're bringing so you can help remind one another about essentials. And if you do forget something, be resourceful. Try not to worry the bride. A call to the wedding planner or maid of honor or even the hotel (or location) staff may provide you with information that can save the day.

Unfortunate Circumstances

When it rains, it pours. You can go months or years with nothing momentous happening in your life, and then you'll suddenly be hit with multiple major events all at once. Unfortunately, the world doesn't stop for any wedding (even though some brides seem to think it should). Things happen that may conflict and cause problems and unfortunately, there's often no way to predict them. As much time as a bride spends planning her perfect event and covering all possible contingencies, there are simply some circumstances that are impossible to predict, like illness, a family emergency, or unreasonable career demands.

 Fact

Even if it's not happening to the bride, groom, or their immediate families, with an entire wedding party on board, there is the potential for some unfortunate circumstance to come into play.

The Social Butterfly

Being a part of a wedding is an honor, but what happens when you commit to be in two weddings without knowing the wedding dates? Well, let's just say chaos may be a good word to use. Take the bridesmaid who was asked to be a bridesmaid in two weddings: neither bride had set her wedding date, and she answered yes to each of the bridesmaid requests, only to soon discover that both weddings would be on the same day—in different cities. What was proper etiquette? And how could she possibly choose without offending one of the brides forever? She prided herself on being a good friend and doing the right thing, so this situation was especially difficult.

If you should find yourself in this situation, you have to carefully consider the relationship with each of the brides. Is one a family member (or future family member)? Is one a long-time, tried-and-true friend? Is one wedding close to home and the other far away? You will have to weigh all of these circumstances and issues as you make a decision. If in fact you find that both brides have equal footing in your world, you will still need to make a decision, but no joke—a flip of the coin may be in order.

ⓔ✳ Essential

As a bridesmaid, a little extra effort can go a long way. This might mean giving a wedding guest a ride to the airport, cat-sitting for the bride while she's on her honeymoon, or creating a "Welcome Home" sign to greet the newlyweds upon their return.

Whatever your decision, one bride is going to have to be told that you will not be walking the aisle with her. Explain the situation honestly, and see what else you might be able to do to help her. Even if you can't fulfill your role as bridesmaid, you can still be there for the bride in other ways, before and/ or after the wedding. Come into the situation with solutions and compromises. Suggest that you still come to her shower and bachelorette party, and maybe offer assistance in planning. Of course, in the short term, the bride may not be that understanding!

The Unavoidable Illness

Sometimes, there is nothing anyone can do about a certain situation. When it comes to an illness, the truth is it just may have to run its course. It is always possible that you or another member of the wedding party may succumb to a bad bug at a most unfortunate time.

 Fact

Bad luck is bad luck, but do your best to ward off an illness. Take good care of yourself the week before the wedding. Get plenty of sleep, avoid other sick people (if possible), and try not to take on too much stressful activity.

Really, how are you going to perform your duties after a rough morning? While fighting off a fever and chills, few people are up for the long walk down the aisle and the event that lies in front of them. Not to mention the fact that being in close proximity to the bathroom is maybe necessary. This is one of those times where your choices are limited, to say the least. If this happens to you, you are just going to have to tell the bride. Of course she'll be disappointed, and you will be as well.

Acts of God

In this big crazy world, events happen that are way beyond the predictable: a terrible snowstorm, a city-wide power outage, or even an act of war. These events are tragic enough when you're going through the motions of day-to-day life, but when they interrupt months of planning and expectations and emotions surrounding a wedding, they're even tougher to handle. The following examples are major catastrophes of different sorts. How they played out are useful examples of how different situations are reacted to and dealt with.

Fallout

Thankfully, tragic events do not happen everyday, but this is yet another thing out of the control of most. In recent memory, one of the most profound events was the September 11th attack. The weekend after September 11, many brides considered canceling their weddings or scaling them back considerably. Not only was the entire country still in shock, but nationwide transportation had been at a standstill for almost three days. These feelings seemed to hit brides on the East Coast especially hard, particularly in New York City. Many families were struggling with the idea of celebrating so soon after all the suffering.

After much consideration, one bride decided to go ahead with the wedding as planned. She and her family called all the out-of-town guests to let them know the wedding would go on, but that the bride and groom would surely understand if they couldn't make it to town. In those uncertain first few days after the attacks, the bride didn't want to make anyone feel as if they had to fly if they didn't feel comfortable with it, or even to leave home and family if they didn't want to.

Most guests felt absolutely compelled to go, in fact. Celebrating life and happiness seemed more important than ever, in the face of so much death and uncertainty. The wedding was very emotional, and the bride couldn't have appreciated the efforts of her guests any more.

Stormy Weather

Weather forecasters can predict nasty weather, but until the storm hits, there is no way of knowing its impact. Of course, as a bride goes about planning her wedding, she has no way of knowing a hurricane will be brewing on her big day. Weather is a fact of life, and unfortunately, you may not know its impact until the wedding or days before the wedding.

The weather can affect the wedding plans in numerous ways. On one hand, it may inhibit you or the guests or even the bride and groom from easily traveling to and from the ceremony and reception site. It may cause delays in the starting time of the ceremony, and wreak havoc on plans for photography and other activities. It can delay public transportation, stop traffic mid-route, and simply leave you stuck without a thing to do.

Essential

Renting a local hotel room or staying with a friend close to the wedding site is a great idea that will save you some stress when it comes to traveling and traffic on the wedding day. Bad weather or traffic jams can create havoc.

The worst-case scenario is that the weather begins a chain of events that leads to a full-blown disaster. Hurricane Katrina is a recent example. The devastation that was caused by the onset of this hurricane brought the Gulf Coast to a standstill and left people fighting for their homes and their lives. A wedding seemed inconsequential then. Just as tragic is the devastation from a tornado or an earthquake.

The moral? Precautions can be taken against acts of God, but weather can be unpredictable. In the simplest terms, don't rely on public transportation, and if you can, sleep as close to the wedding site as you can get. However, as recent events have shown the world, there are times when there is nothing anyone can do. At these moments when nothing can be done, you have to deal with the hand life has given you.

Girls Will Be Girls

Whereas guys can virtually ignore each other, verbally abuse each other, and even get in fistfights and remain best friends, girls make it a bit more difficult on each other. Failing to return a phone call can become a major offense. Neglecting to show up to a promised event can be a total deal-breaker. Then there are the more subtle transgressions, like not being excited enough when a friend reports good news or those sly put-downs that only a friend could recognize.

Unfortunately, these kinds of subtle offenses can become monumental when they surround a wedding. Possibly, it's because they're infused with so many expectations and so much symbolism. There are some women who keep a mental tally of their "bridesmaid list" throughout their lives as a way of defining their ongoing relationships with other women. This list inevitably changes from the teen years until the day she gets married, but it never loses its significance—a declaration to the world of the women the bride considers her favorite people, her best friends.

That's why being asked to be a bridesmaid can be such an honor, and not being asked can be so hurtful. It's also why failure to live up to one's bridesmaid duties can be so offensive. The bride feels she's put her public trust in you. If you should fail to live up to it, it's proof that you don't care much about her or your relationship. It's complicated being a woman.

Bridesmaid for Hire

You have probably heard not to ever mix business and pleasure. This holds true for the wedding party! Despite anyone's best intentions, some things should not happen. Such was the case of one generous and thoughtful bride who was always trying to help her friends out. One of the bridesmaids was launching a floral business, and the bride thought hiring her friend would be a wonderful way to show her support, so she asked the bridesmaid to design her wedding flowers. The bridesmaid was not skilled enough or ready to take on a job of this magnitude, but agreed anyway.

e! Alert

> Be a bridesmaid or be a vendor. Being both is exceptionally hard on you and on the bride, as neither job gets its full attention.

Not only was this lady serving as bridesmaid and expected to attend all prewedding festivities, she also had the burden of providing beautiful flowers for the wedding when she was not equipped to handle the job. Ultimately, the bridesmaid was up all night trying to complete the floral work for the wedding. And, ultimately, the flowers were not done. They were eventually dropped off at the wedding location two-thirds done, but that was all she could do.

The High-Maintenance Monster

Unfortunately, you can be a perfect bridesmaid and still be abused. As mentioned earlier, some women change when they get that ring on their finger. Something takes over, and it is called "Bridezilla." It may be temporary . . . it may be permanent . . . but it is often irrational. In a case like this, no matter how helpful and supportive you are, you will still be "wrong."

Take the case of the bridesmaid who thought she was reconnecting with a childhood friend. The bridesmaid had done everything she was supposed to. She helped plan a shower from afar, attended the shower and the bachelorette party in another city, ordered her dress on time, and e-mailed or called the bride at least once a week to provide a little moral support.

That was not enough for this high-maintenance bride; nothing would have been good enough. She was offended that the bridesmaid hadn't attended two additional showers that had been thrown for her. While she couldn't make those, she had sent gifts. The bride was upset that the bridesmaid, with a demanding work schedule, couldn't come to town a few days before the wedding to help with last-minute details.

ⓔ✔ Fact

As a bridesmaid, it's your duty to attend all prewedding parties. However, if they're all out of town, there's an exception to the rule. If you can't attend all of them, talk to the bride to see whether she'd prefer you at any one or two specific events.

You don't have to be a doormat. While you should fulfill your bridesmaid duties and try to go beyond them in the name of friendship, you can only do your best. If the bride resents that, it may be time to re-evaluate the friendship.

The Bridesmaid Who Never Was

Sometimes being asked to be a bridesmaid can be a dreaded obligation—the cost, the travel, and the effort may seem burdensome. Even so, not being asked can be an even worse blow. After all, if you're not asked to be a friend's bridesmaid, and you were totally expecting it, it can throw your entire sense of perception into a tailspin. Does this person not value me? Have I done something to offend her? Have I been living in a dream world, believing we were much closer than we are? These are some of the questions you may have when snubbed from bridesmaid duty.

 Alert

> If you haven't been asked to be a bridesmaid and you have other friends who have, try not to put them in the middle of the situation. While it may be tempting to solicit their allegiance, they're also trying to be sincere participants in the upcoming nuptials.

Then there are those friendships that you recognize have been on the rocks. You hope you'll be asked to be a bridesmaid nonetheless, as a good-faith gesture toward reconciliation, for old times' sake, or even simply because the rest of your group of friends will be bridesmaids and you don't want to miss out on the fun. On top of all that, to be publicly rejected is embarrassing. No matter what the reasons, being overlooked as a bridesmaid can bring back those awful, primal grade school feelings again, like when your fifth-grade best friend suddenly found a new one.

The Nonbridesmaid

One nonbridesmaid, stung that she wasn't asked to be a part of her college girlfriend's wedding party, decided to shun the wedding completely. She felt especially hurt because the bride had been a bridesmaid in her wedding just two years before. The reasons she was ignored are as layered as a wedding cake—years of perceived wrongs against each other had resulted in hard feelings and a lack of communication, and they'd simply drifted apart without ever hashing out their problems.

While they still ran into each other at the social functions of mutual friends, there was definitely some long-term resentment that had built. For the nonbridesmaid, not being asked was the last straw in an already tenuous friendship. She decided that she'd be uncomfortable attending the prewedding events and the wedding itself, so she didn't.

Low Key and Relaxed

Believe it or not, there are brides whose dreams do not include big bridal parties and fancy weddings. There really are brides who only want a bridesmaid or two; they prefer low key and close knit. However, when these feelings and desires are not known or addressed, they can lead to hurt feelings. Even when these brides have not meant to snub anyone, it may seem that way. Rather, they have made a personal decision about how to manage their wedding.

If you find yourself in this situation, the best bet is to just be honest and talk to the bride. Often, open communication can make all the difference in salvaging a relationship and easing hard feelings. If you're feeling hurt about being excluded from a friend's wedding party and the friendship is worth it to you, talk to the bride. If it's the last straw in an already declining friendship, it may simply be time to cut your losses. It could also be a clue to treat this relationship in accordance—as a more casual friendship or acquaintance.

The Drama Queen

We all know the type. It's amazing, in fact, how the tilt of the earth's axis is so tied to her every move. No matter what the occasion, it's all about her. No matter what anyone's problem, she's got one to top it. And no matter how funny the story, she's got one that's funnier. And while she may be irritating, she can also be a good friend. That's the reason a bride may choose just this type to be one of her bridesmaids, despite some of her selfish habits.

Of course, the bride should have expected that not everything would go smoothly. During the engagement, the bridesmaid first had a messy breakup with her boyfriend. In a dramatic scene, she described the breakup in great detail to anyone who'd listen, and that she also quit her job—threw a glass of water in her boss's face, to be precise. At every prewedding event, the party quickly seemed to become less about celebrating the bride and more about attending to the bridesmaid. Due to her innate self-involvement, she never even noticed she was stealing the spotlight from the bride with her myriad dramas, stories, and complaints.

Essential

Try not to demand too much attention at the wedding or prewedding events; it's the bride's turn to bask in the spotlight. She shouldn't have to share it, for better or worse, with you.

Does this describe you? Come on; be honest with yourself! If so, keep it and your drama or larger-than-life personality in check. Behave and be respectful. Try not to steal the spotlight from the bride at any wedding-related events. This means saving big announcements for a more suitable time and behaving like a respectable person. Let someone else bask in the attention for once.

A Family Affair

Even in the most harmonious of families, some sticky situations can arise while planning and hosting a wedding. When it comes to mixing bridesmaid and family issues, it's best to err on the side of caution. This is true for circumstances ranging from deciding whether or not to accept a bridesmaid post from your future sister-in-law to dealing with being the unmarried maid of honor for your little sister. The following scenarios illustrate some difficult family affairs bridesmaids have faced, and how they got through them intact.

Touchy Situation

Jane dated the bride's brother. They broke up. She moved on; he didn't. Now, a few years later, the bride asked Jane to be a bridesmaid. The brother saw this as a chance to rekindle a relationship, and when he found out that it would not happen, he became angry and aggressive. He wanted the bride to "un-ask" Jane, but she wouldn't dream of it. He said he would not be a part of the wedding. Not a pretty picture, eh?

What to do? Jane wondered if she should pull out of the proceedings or honor her commitment to the bride. When all seems irrational, like in this situation, you should look for help. Jane asked the mother to step in and talk some sense into her son. The last thing the bride needed was to be thrust into this situation. Fortunately, mom intervened with a brutally honest sit-down with the brother. Because it was put into perspective by an "outside" source, tragedy was averted. If being a bridesmaid threatens to compromise certain allegiances, take diplomatic action rather than ignoring the situation.

Assumed and Ignored

When two families come together, there are, of course, different ways of doing things. When one lady's younger brother got engaged, she couldn't have been happier. She had heard his fiancée was a lovely person, though she'd never met her—the two lived across the country and had been dating for less than a year. As the engagement period went on, she waited for the phone call asking her to be bridesmaid—she was the groom's sister, of course she would be included . . . right?

As time went on, the phone didn't ring. She realized that a request might not be forthcoming. She asked her mother, and still no word. Finally, she questioned her brother. Her brother informed her that the bride had asked her two sisters and her best friend, for a total of three bridesmaids. They didn't want to go overboard with the size of their wedding party, and because they'd never met, the bride didn't feel comfortable asking her.

Fact

There is no obligation, as dictated by etiquette, that requires siblings to be included in the wedding party. While it may make peace in the family, the decision it ultimately up to the bride and groom.

Both sides misunderstood the situation and it continued to escalate. Then the groom's mother jumped in; she was equally outraged that her daughter wouldn't be included in the wedding party. When they finally all came together for the couple's engagement party a month later, the situation was definitely tense. The groom's mother and sister did not extend the bride a very warm welcome to the family, and it made the bride feel sad and uncomfortable.

To salve the bruised egos, the bride went ahead and asked the groom's sister to take part in the wedding. To the bride, it seemed that this gesture might be too little, too late, but the groom's sister was pleased as punch, and all was harmonious again.

Don't extrapolate your behavior onto everyone else. Just because you would ask your ten best friends and three coworkers to take part in your wedding doesn't mean everyone else would, too. If you haven't been asked to be a bridesmaid, try to put yourself in the bride's shoes before becoming paranoid and/or taking it personally. If you still feel it's an unjustified snub, try to get to the bottom of the situation.

Question

I don't have a boyfriend right now. Should I bring a random date to the wedding?

Just a date may not be the best idea. You'll be busy, and he presumably won't know anyone. You may end up feeling obliged to entertain him, which could distract you from your bridesmaid duties or your own good time. Go solo, and have fun.

Always a Bridesmaid

What happens when your little sister gets engaged . . . and you are still single? Of course, there is happiness, but it is quite likely this will raise some feelings and uneasiness about your own situation. As plans progress, it may only get worse.

Chances are as the older, unmarried sister, you will be on the receiving end of insensitive questions from some of the older relatives: "Well, what about you? When are you getting married?" As if it wasn't bad enough dealing with being single with no current prospects, now you have to deal with it publicly, and prominently dateless at the wedding.

Things don't always work out on a timeline of our choosing. If you're feeling down about being single while your friend or family member is blissfully engaged, remember that your day will come, too. Don't fret! As a bridesmaid, you will be busy greeting family and friends and helping your sister—no time for a date, anyway! Try, hard as it may be, to bask in the residual joy of the bride's happiness.

Appendix: Worksheets

The Bridesmaid Roster

MAID/MATRON OF HONOR: _____
Phone/Cell Phone: _____
E-mail: _____
Address: _____
Twitter: _____

BRIDESMAID: _____
Phone/Cell Phone: _____
E-mail: _____
Address: _____
Twitter: _____

BRIDESMAID: _____
Phone/Cell Phone: _____
E-mail: _____
Address: _____
Twitter: _____

BRIDESMAID: _____
Phone/Cell Phone: _____
E-mail: _____
Address: _____
Twitter: _____

BRIDESMAID: _____
Phone/Cell Phone: _____
E-mail: _____
Address: _____
Twitter: _____

BRIDESMAID: _____

Phone/Cell Phone: _____

E-mail: _____

Address: _____

Twitter: _____

BRIDESMAID: _____

Phone/Cell Phone: _____

E-mail: _____

Address: _____

Twitter: _____

FLOWER GIRL: _____

Parents' Names: _____

Phone/Cell Phone: _____

E-mail: _____

Address: _____

Bridesmaids' Attire

STORE WHERE PURCHASED: _____

Address: _____

Telephone: _____

Store hours: _____

Directions: _____

Salesperson: _____

DESCRIPTION OF DRESS

Manufacturer: _____

Style number: _____

Color: _____

Dress size: _____

Total cost of dress: _____

Deposit paid: _____

Balance due: _____

Delivery date: _____

Fitting date #1: _____

          Time: _____

Fitting date #2: _____

          Time: _____

Fitting date #3: _____

          Time: _____

Cost of alterations: _____

DESCRIPTION OF SHOES

Store where purchased: _____

Manufacturer: _____

Style number: _____

Size: _____

Color: _____

DESCRIPTION OF ACCESSORIES

Gloves: _____

Store where purchased: _____

Hosiery: _____

Store where purchased: _____

Jewelry: _____

Store where purchased: _____

Important Dates

Use this to keep track of the important dates related to wedding events.

Wedding date: _____

Rehearsal dinner: _____

Bridesmaids' luncheon: _____

Bridesmaids' shower: _____

Other shower: _____

Bachelorette party: _____

Bachelor party: _____

Engagement party: _____

Shower Guest List

Name: _____

Address: _____

Telephone: _____

❑   RSVP

Name: _____

Address: _____

Telephone: _____

❑   RSVP

Name: _____

Address: _____

Telephone: _____

❑   RSVP

Name: _____
Address: _____
Telephone: _____

❏   RSVP

Name: _____
Address: _____
Telephone: _____

❏   RSVP

Name: _____
Address: _____
Telephone: _____

❏   RSVP

Name: _____
Address: _____
Telephone: _____

❏   RSVP

Name: _____
Address: _____
Telephone: _____

❏   RSVP

Name: _____
Address: _____
Telephone: _____

❏   RSVP

Name: _____
Address: _____
Telephone: _____

❑   RSVP

Name: _____
Address: _____
Telephone: _____

❑   RSVP

Shower Planning Checklist

Three (or more) months before:
   ❑ Decide on type of shower
   ❑ Decide on time of day
   ❑ Choose a location
   ❑ Set a date
   ❑ Set a budget
   ❑ Compile guest list
   ❑ Select caterer
   ❑ Select florist
   ❑ Shop for and order party favors
   ❑ Reserve space for shower (if applicable)

Six weeks before:
   ❑ Confirm time and date with caterer
   ❑ Confirm time and date with florist
   ❑ Send out invitations

Five weeks before:

❑ Begin recording guest responses

Four weeks before:

❑ Finalize details with caterer
❑ Finalize details with florist
❑ Purchase shower gift for bride

One week before:

❑ Finalize number of guests with caterer OR
❑ Shop for liquor and nonperishables (if throwing shower yourself)
❑ Plan seating arrangements
❑ Pick up and arrange shower favors

A few days before:

❑ Begin preparing food

Shower Budget

Item	Description	Projected Cost	Actual Cost	Balance Due
Space rental				
Caterer				
Food and liquor costs (if throwing at home)				
Flowers/decorations				
Shower favors				
Prizes for shower games				
Gift for the bride				
Other items:				

Shower Gift List		
Description of gift	Gift-giver's name	Thank-you note sent

Bachelorette Party Guest List

Name: _____

Address: _____

Telephone: _____

❏   RSVP

Name: _____

Address: _____

Telephone: _____

❏   RSVP

Name: _____

Address: _____

Telephone: _____

❏   RSVP

Name: _____

Address: _____

Telephone: _____

❏   RSVP

Name: _____

Address: _____

Telephone: _____

❏   RSVP

Name: _____
Address: _____
Telephone: _____

❏ RSVP

Name: _____
Address: _____
Telephone: _____

❏ RSVP

Name: _____
Address: _____
Telephone: _____

❏ RSVP

Name: _____
Address: _____
Telephone: _____

❏ RSVP

Name: _____
Address: _____
Telephone: _____

❏ RSVP

Name: _____
Address: _____
Telephone: _____

❏ RSVP

Name: _____

Address: _____

Telephone: _____

❏   RSVP

Bachelorette Party Checklist

Three (or more) months before:

❏ Decide on type of bachelorette party

❏ Decide on time of day

❏ Choose a location

❏ Set a date

❏ Set a budget

❏ Compile guest list

❏ Begin pricing transportation options, such as limos

❏ Begin shopping for party props (especially if ordering online)

Six weeks before:

❏ Make reservations at a restaurant or club, if applicable

❏ Order and put deposit down on transportation or limousine service

❏ Order and put deposit down on entertainment

❏ Send out invitations or begin getting the word out via e-mail or phone

Four weeks before:

❏ Make final bachelorette goody and game purchases

One week before:

- ❑ Confirm limo and entertainment services
- ❑ Shop for liquor and nonperishables (if throwing party yourself)
- ❑ Send out e-mail reminder to all those attending

A few days before:

- ❑ Shop for perishable items
- ❑ Make any food you can ahead of time
- ❑ Clean your house

Bachelorette Party Budget

Item	Description	Projected Cost	Actual Cost	Balance Due
Limo or transportation rental				
Dinner				
Food and liquor costs (if throwing party at home)				
Decorations/bachelorette props				
Stripper				
Games and prizes				
Gift for bride				
Other items:				

Index

ABC shower, 105

Absent bridesmaid, tips for
    handling, 90

Accessories
    costs and, 50–51
    styles and, 70

Activity shower, 109–10

Alcohol, limiting
    consumption of, 230–32

Alterations to dress, costs of,
    49–50

Aromatherapy, to calm bride,
    181

Bachelorette party, 121–43
    basics of, 122–23
    costs of, 122, 123–24,
        137–38
    entertainment for, 164–67
    games for, 157–63
    guests at, 129–32
    maid of honor's
        responsibility for, 32–33
    planning for, 125–29
    props for games at, 162–63
    for second wedding,
        213–14
    themes for, 132–43
    worksheets for, 253–58

Bad news, keeping to self,
    182

Big Night Out, for
    bachelorette party, 132–33
    games for, 159–61

Bingo game, 149

Bitchy bridesmaid, tips for
    handling, 90

Bouquet(s)
    for maid of honor and
        bridesmaids, 39
    toss of bride's, 206–7

Boyfriend, of bridesmaid
    breakup and, 220
    emotions of wedding and,
        81–84

Breakfast, on wedding day,
    191

Breathing exercises, for
    nervous bride, 182

Bridal Bingo game, 149

Bridal quiz show, 154–55

Bridal registries, 186–87

Bridal shower, 93–119
    activities for, 153–57
    basics of, 95
    costs of, 53–54, 98–99
    games for, 146–53
    guests at, 113–18
    history of, 94
    maid of honor and, 31–32,
        36–37
    non-game activities for,
        153–57
    planning for, 96–98,
        100–104
    for second wedding, 213,
        214
    themes for, 104–13

worksheets for, 259–63
Bride
    bachelorette party
      planning and, 126–29
    bridal shower planning
      and, 102–3
    bridesmaid
      disagreements and, 91
    evaluating personality of,
      7–10
    games at shower and, 153
    handling high-
      maintenance, 240–41
    maid of honor as liaison
      for, 30
    not competing with, 78
    postwedding friendship
      and, 223–28
Bridesmaid(s)
    avoiding multiple
      responsibilities on
      wedding day, 239–40
    Bridesmaid Quotient test,
      14–17
    duties and roles of, 4–6, 10
    emotions and, 81–84
    expected attendance and
      gifts at bridal showers,
      104, 112
    family issues and, 245–48
    for groom, 214–16
    handling dilemmas of,
      219–23, 234–48
    history of, 2–4

    maid of honor's
      responsibility to
      communicate with,
      26–27
    maid of honor's
      responsibility to
      organize, 28–29, 39
    preventable foibles of,
      230–33
    reacting to being asked to
      be, 11–14
    reacting to not being
      asked to be, 240–44,
      246–47
    saying no gracefully, 10,
      17–21
    shower guest list and,
      113–14
    special circumstances
      and, 73–92
    stress relief for, 184–85
    tips for handling conflict
      with other, 87–92
    what to pay for, 48–49, 71
    worksheets for, 71, 250–52
Bridesmaids' luncheon, 37
Bridezilla, tips for handling,
    84–87
Broke bridesmaid, tips for
    handling, 91
Budget-conscious wedding
    costs, 55–57

Cancelled wedding, 216–19

Ceremony
  behavior during, 197–98,
    200–201
  maid of honor and, 40
  receiving line after, 201–2
  walking down aisle, 198–
    200, 201
Checklists. *See* Worksheets
  and checklists
Coed bachelorette party,
  140–41
Comedy club visit, for
  bachelorette party,
  134–135
Couples shower, 110–12
Creative gifts, ideas for,
  187–88

Dance, of bridal party, 205–6
Dares, bachelorette party
  game of, 160
Death in family, tips for
  bridesmaid's handling of,
  222–23
Decadence theme, for
  bachelorette party, 137
Designer wedding costs,
  57–58
Destination wedding costs,
  63–65
Dress, for bride
  maid of honor and, 34
  picking up, 176
Dress, for bridesmaids

bride's choice and, 17, 67
cancelled wedding and,
  217–18
costs and, 49–50
current trends in, 65–66
final fitting for, 176
having ready, 232–33
individual choice and,
  66–67, 69
maid of honor and, 34–35
pregnancy and, 76–77
styles, lengths, and fabrics,
  67–69
wearing again, 69

E-mail, to other bridesmaids,
  88
Emergency kit, for bride,
  183–84
Engagement party, 36
Expenses. *See* Financial
  issues

Facebook page, 29
Family issues
  bridesmaid's obligations
    to own family, 221–22
  brother's fiancé and,
    246–47
  dating bride's brother, 245
Famous Couple Trivia game,
  152
Financial issues
  bachelorette party, 122,

123–24, 137–38
bridal shower, 98–99
bridesmaids dresses and
    accessories, 35, 65–71
broke bridesmaid, 91
decisions about being
    bridesmaid, 13, 19–20
multiple weddings, 80–81
style and scale of
    wedding, 55–65
ways to economize, 49–55
First Kiss game, 158
First year of marriage,
    friendship with bride and,
    223–28
Fitness shower, 105–6

Games, 145–67
    for bachelorette party,
        157–63
    basics of, 146–48
    for bridal shower, 146–53
    prizes for, 147–48
    props for, 162–63
Garter toss, 207–8, 209
Gifts
    for bachelorette party, 137
    for bridal shower, 118
    costs of, 54–55, 57
    keeping track of, 119, 258
    for wedding, 185–88
Gift basket and story, as
    shower game, 156–57
Groom

bachelorette party
    game about bride's
        knowledge of, 158–59
    bridal quiz show game
        and, 155
    getting along with, 224,
        227
Groomswoman, 214–16
Guess the Goodies game, 151
Guests, at bachelorette party
    being hostess to, 129–30
    mothers, 129
    worksheets and checklists
        for, 131, 259–61
Guests, at bridal shower,
    113–18
    worksheets and checklists
        for, 115–16, 253–55

Hair styling costs, 51, 70–71
Hobby shower, 106
Holiday shower, 108–9
Home-based bachelorette
    parties, 135–40
Hotels
    amenities for bride at, 174
    costs of accommodations
        at, 53
House party, for bachelorette
    party, 135–37
    games for, 158–59

Illness, tips for bridesmaid's
    handling of, 222, 235–36

Indifferent bridesmaid, tips
for handling, 88
I Never game, 159
In-town wedding costs, 58–59
Invitations, for bridal shower,
113, 117–18

Job loss, tips for bridesmaid's
handling of, 220

Lingerie shower, 106–7
Luncheon, for bridesmaids,
170–71

Maid of honor, 2, 23–45
bachelorette party, 123
bridesmaid
disagreements and, 92
expectations of, 24–25
having two, 25–26
responsibilities before
wedding day, 26–37, 233
responsibilities on
wedding day, 38–45
Makeup, professional, 71
Marriage, offering tips to
bride, as shower game,
155
Massage, to calm bride, 180
Memories, recounting
funniest about bride, at
shower, 155
Memory game, 152
Men

at bachelorette party,
131–32, 140–41
as bridal attendants, 7, 66,
214–16
at couples shower, 110–12
Mish-Mash Marriage game,
151
Mother of bride, help with
Bridezilla, 87
Moving away, tips for
bridesmaid's handling of,
220–21
Multiple weddings
choosing between, 79–80,
234–35
expenses and, 80–81
Mummy Bride game, 153

Newly engaged bridesmaid,
responsibilities and, 77–78
Newlyweds, respecting
privacy of, 209

Out-of-town visitors, helping
bride with arrangements
for, 175–76, 178
Out-of-town wedding costs,
59–60

Parties. See Bachelorette
party; Bridal shower
Photographs
of games, 151
maid of honor and, 39, 41

preparing for wedding
day, 194–96
tips for looking your best
in, 196–97
Pin It on the Groom game,
152
Pin the Tail on the Man
game, 158
Poker party theme, for
bachelorette party,
139–40
Pregnancy
bridesmaid
responsibilities and,
74–77
and decisions about
accepting or declining
bridesmaid invitation,
18–19
Pre-wedding activities, 169–
88. *See also* Bachelorette
party; Bridal shower
assisting bride, 175–78
bridesmaid's lunch,
170–71
gift selection, 185–88
rehearsal dinner, 173–75
stress relief for bride,
178–85
wedding rehearsal,
171–73
Prizes, for games, 147–48
Props, for games, 162–63
Purse game, 150–51

Quarrel with bride, tips for
handling, 221

Receiving line, 41, 201–2
Reception
behavior during, 203
bouquet toss, 206–7
bridal party dance, 205–6
duties during, 203–4
garter toss, 207–8, 209
maid of honor and,
41–45
seating during, 204–5
toasts, 43–44, 206, 207
Recipe shower, 112–13
Rehearsal, for wedding,
171–73
Rehearsal dinner, 37, 173–75,
190
"Right Date" game, 150

Safety-Pin game, 150
Salon appointments, 177,
191–93
Scavenger Hunt, at
bachelorette party, 160–61
Scrapbook, creating at bridal
shower, 154
Second weddings, 212–14
September 11 attack, 237
Shoes
breaking in, 200
costs and, 50
Shower. *See* Bridal shower

Sister, handling engagement of younger, 247–48

Sleep, importance of, 190–91, 195

Slumber party, for bachelorette party, 138–39

Snacks, for bride, 181

Sophisticated dinner, for bachelorette party, 133–34

South-of-the Border theme, for bachelorette party, 136

Spa treatment, to calm bride, 180

Spice Girls game, 150

Sports-related bachelorette party, 142–43

Stress, helping relieve bride's, 178–85

Strip club, bachelorette party at, 167

Stripper, for bachelorette party, 164–66

Suck for a Buck game, 159–60

Take-control bridesmaid, tips for handling, 89

Tea, for bridesmaids, 170–71

Themes, for bachelorette party, 132–43
    Big Night Out, 132–33
    coed part, 140–41
    comedy club visit, 134–35
    house party, 135–37

poker party, 139–40
slumber party, 138–39
sophisticated dinner, 133–34
sports-related events, 142–43
weekend getaway, 141–42

Themes, for bridal shower, 104–13
    ABC shower, 105
    activity shower, 109–10
    couples shower, 110–12
    fitness shower, 105–6
    hobby shower, 106
    holiday shower, 108–9
    including on invitations, 118
    lingerie shower, 106–7
    recipe shower, 112–13
    wine shower, 109

Theme wedding costs, 61–63

Toasts, at reception, 43–44, 206, 207

Travel distance
    costs and, 51–52
    decisions about being bridesmaid, 20
    time and, 192

Troubled bridesmaid, tips for handling, 89–90

Twitter, 29

Unexpected events, handling of, 237

Very Daring game, 160

Weather
effect of alcohol
consumption and,
231–32
wedding plans and
unexpected, 237–38
Wedding, costs of various
styles of, 55–65
Wedding day, 189–209
ceremony, 197–201
emergency kit for, 183–84
photographs and, 194–97
post-ceremony, 201–3
post-reception, 208–9
preparation for, 190–93
reception, 203–8
relaxing before ceremony,
193–94
Wedding favors, helping
bride with, 177–78
Wedding Song game, 149
Weekend getaway, for
bachelorette party, 141–42
Whatcha playing? game,
148–49
Wine shower, 109
Wine tasting, for
bachelorette party, 136–37
Worksheets and checklists
bachelorette party
budget, 263
bachelorette party guests,
131, 259–61
bachelorette party
planning, 261–63
bridal shower budget, 257
bridal shower gifts, 119,
258
bridal shower guests,
115–16, 253–55
bridal shower planning,
96–98, 255–56
bridesmaids' attire, 251–52
bridesmaids' roster,
250–51
important dates, 253

Find out Everything on Anything at **everything.com!**

At **Everything.com** you can explore thousands of articles on hundreds of topics—from starting your own business and personal finance to health-care advice and help with parenting, cooking, learning a new language, and more. And you also can:

- **Share advice**
- **Rate articles**
- **Submit articles**
- **Sign up for our Everything.com newsletters**

Visit **Everything.com** where you'll find the broadest range and most authoritative content available online!